The New Start-up Plan

By

Nicholas Todd Rustad, MBA

V6

Copyright © 2024 by Nicholas T. Rustad, MBA
All rights reserved.

Copyright © 2024 by Nicholas Todd Rustad, MBA. All rights reserved.

No part of this publication may be reproduced, distributed, or transmitted in any form or by any means, including photocopying, recording, or other electronic or mechanical methods, without the prior written permission of the copyright owner, except in the case of brief quotations embodied in critical reviews and certain other non-commercial uses permitted by copyright law.

DISCLAIMER: The information provided in this book is based on the experience of Nicholas and his team at CoreTactic LLC and is not intended to be a substitute for professional advice from a legal, financial, or medical expert. CoreTactic and Nicholas Rustad are not liable for any use of this information.

In this book I will going to detail how I created our start-up, CoreTactic, and all that goes into such an adventure. Included are many caution statements in this material, and it is important that you pay attention to the danger areas before you jump into starting a company. Sprinkled throughout this book will also be key blog posts that I have created over the last year, to help bind the story together. In addition, I will provide some legal, medical, or financial information and if you are starting a company, hire a lawyer, accountant and/or therapist. The material in this book should not be considered professional legal, medical, or financial advice. There is no substitute for an expert. In addition, if you see * that is denoted that the information came from a reference, and you can find the references in the appendix. Enjoy the book!

Copyright © 2024 by Nicholas T. Rustad, MBA
All rights reserved.

Thank You

Primarily, I owe an immense debt of gratitude to many individuals who have played pivotal roles in my journey. Of course, the love of my life Travis, David P., Marisa, John S., Greg, Andrea, Sara E., George, Ruth, David D., and Jennfier O. have been unwavering pillars of support and encouragement throughout my life. Also, thank you to our whole CoreTactic team of Renee, Vanessa, Jenny, Eric, Travis, Ruth, Elizabeth, Jaime, Jeffory, Joe, Lucy, Sean, Anne, Elena, and so many others. Their advice, attentive listening, and valuable suggestions have been instrumental in shaping my path.

Dad imparted invaluable lessons in technology, strategy, and critical thinking, while mom instilled in me the principles of exceptional customer service, compassion for others, and the essence of leadership. Their unwavering support, despite the absence of extended family backing, was a cornerstone of my success.

Copyright © 2024 by Nicholas T. Rustad, MBA
All rights reserved.

Foreword

In "The New Start-up Plan" author Nicholas Todd Rustad, MBA, CSM, CSPO shares an inspiring tale of resilience, transformation, and entrepreneurial triumph. Drawing from his own remarkable journey, Nicholas takes you on a captivating ride through the difficulties of starting and growing a successful business.

This book is not just a guide to entrepreneurship; it is a testament to the human spirit's capacity for innovation and adaptability. Nicholas's story begins in a small northern Minnesota town, where he defied the odds to become the first in his family to earn both an undergraduate degree and an MBA.

With over 25 years of corporate experience and as the founder of CoreTactic, a thriving organization, Nicholas has faced challenges head-on.

"The New Start-up Plan" offers invaluable insights for aspiring entrepreneurs and seasoned business owners alike. Nicholas shares his strategies for discovering your passion, connecting with your target audience, marketing your offerings, managing finances, and building a thriving enterprise.

Join Nick on an extraordinary journey of transformation and discover how to not only survive but thrive in the face of adversity. This start-up story is a beacon of hope and a guide to turning life's challenges into opportunities for something utterly amazing.

Copyright © 2024 by Nicholas T. Rustad, MBA
All rights reserved.

Table of Contents

CHAPTER 1: START-UP BIRTH 1
    REALITY 2
    RENAISSANCE WEB CONSULTING 3
    BLOG POST 4
    BUILD A TEAM 5
    MARKETING AND GROWTH 6
    MONITOR AND ADAPT 6
    SCALE YOUR BUSINESS 7
    DEVELOP AND LAUNCH 7
    FINDING FLOW? 7
    HANDLING STRESS AND ANXIETY 8
    DEALING WITH IMPOSTER SYNDROME 9
    THE BUSINESS PLAN 10
    WRITING A COMPREHENSIVE BUSINESS PLAN 11

CHAPTER 2: BANKS AND LAWS 15
    ESTABLISHING A BUSINESS 16
    SECURING BUSINESS INSURANCE 16
    FINANCIAL PLANNING FOR YOUR BUSINESS 20
    BLOG POST 23

CHAPTER 3: START-UP DEATH 28
    STATISTICS 29
    HOW TO BE A GOOD BOSS 30
    RESCUING YOUR START-UP 33
    LEVERAGING CUSTOMER FEEDBACK 34
    BLOG POST 39

CHAPTER 4: START-UP RE-BIRTH 43

Copyright © 2024 by Nicholas T. Rustad, MBA
All rights reserved.

FAILURE OR RE-BIRTH.. 44

GO BACK TO BASICS 44

PAYMENT COLLECTION SYSTEM 45

BLOG POST 50

CHAPTER 5: START COOKING 54

COMPLIANCE 55

BUDGETING FOR SUCCESS 56

WARNING: POTENTIAL SITUATION 59

TAXATION 60

DOCUMENTATION REQUIREMENTS 63

CHAPTER 6: SUSTAINABILITY 65

DIVERSIFICATION 66

MARKET DIVERSIFICATION 67

INCOME DIVERSIFICATION 68

CHAPTER 7: SOURCING CLIENT LEADS 72

SEARCH ENGINE OPTIMIZATION (SEO) 74

EMAIL MARKETING 74

NURTURING LEADS AND BUILDING TRUST 75

CONVERTING AND RETAINING CLIENTS 75

ONLINE ADVERTISING 77

SOCIAL MEDIA 78

NETWORKING 78

BLOG POST 80

CHAPTER 8: STAY OUT OF JAIL 84

LIABILITY 85

DOCUMENTATION 88

DATA SECURITY MEASURES 88

MONITOR CLIENT STATUS 89

Copyright © 2024 by Nicholas T. Rustad, MBA
All rights reserved.

ABSENCE OF CONTRACTS 89
DISSATISFACTION 91
LEGAL EXPERTISE 92
COMPREHENSIVE COVERAGE 92
TAILORED AGREEMENTS 92
WARNING: POTENTIAL SITUATION 94
INTEGRATION WITH ONLINE BOOKING 94
THE TRANSFORMATIVE IMPACT 94
IMPROVED FINANCIAL STABILITY 95
STREAMLINED OPERATIONS 95
LEGAL PROTECTION 95
INSURANCE AND INDEMNITY 96
THE CRUCIAL LESSON LEARNED 97
EXTENSIVE RESEARCH 97
INTELLECTUAL PROPERTY 99
CONTRACTS AND AGREEMENTS 100

CHAPTER 9: PUSH 104

INNOVATION 105
PERSISTENCE 109
BLOG POST 111
THE POWER OF AI TECHNOLOGY 111
PREPARING FOR THE AI FUTURE 112
CAN AI HELP ME START A BUSINESS? 113

FINAL THOUGHTS 115

APPENDIX A: 118
APPENDIX B: 125
ABOUT THE AUTHOR 128
INSPIRATION BEHIND CORETACTIC 130
FREEBEES! 131

Copyright © 2024 by Nicholas T. Rustad, MBA
All rights reserved.

Chapter 1: start-up Birth

ROCK n' ROLL! You made a smart and sometimes scary decision to start your own business! Congrats, step one done and many more to go, but you can do it!

When you decide to start your own business, it is important to have a clear idea of what you want to do and how you plan to do it. Also, you will want to think about what will make your business so unique, that it is hard to copy. While I was in graduate school, I had an amazing professor that talked about how our business must be inimitable, which means so unique it is hard or impossible to copy.

> *"Whatever you do, be different – that was the advice my mother gave me, and I can't think of better advice for an entrepreneur. If you're different, you will stand out." –*
> *Anita Roddick, founder of The Body Shop*

Reality

Now a story of the harsh reality. When trying to start your own business and make enough money to sustain you, it can be virtually impossible. While not completely impossible, it is going to take a certain amount of skill, resources, investment, and a lot of feedback to get it going in the right direction.

Renaissance Web Consulting

Thinking back to the 1990s when I was in a relationship with someone who wanted to start a business. We wanted to start the business because we did not want to go to work anymore and we thought buying two computers and two desks, some notepads and a couple phones would make us money. Plus, we had an extra phone line installed in the house, and then poof, we thought, money would come pouring in! We had a great idea for the business, and back in 1999, if we had had the experience, we could have turned into millionaires.

The business was called Renaissance Web Consulting, and I were going to provide tech support and web design solutions to local clients in the Twin Cities. This is a little homage to my friend Mike!

BLOG POST

How to Start a start-up: A Comprehensive Guide

Launching a start-up is an exciting and challenging journey that requires careful planning, dedication, and a willingness to take risks. While the road to success is often paved with obstacles, the rewards of creating a successful start-up can be both financially and personally fulfilling. In this blog post, I will provide you with a comprehensive guide on how to start a start-up, from idea generation to scaling your business.

Idea Generation

The first step in starting a start-up is to produce a compelling idea. Your idea should address a specific problem or need in the market. Here are a couple tips for generating start-up ideas:

Identify pain points: Look for common problems or challenges that people face in their daily lives or industries.

Market research: Conduct thorough market research to understand current trends, consumer behaviour, and competition.

Passion and expertise: Consider your own interests and expertise. Building a start-up around something you are passionate about can be motivating.

Innovation: Think about how you can offer a unique solution or improve upon existing products or services.

> *"It's not about ideas. It's about making ideas happen."* — Scott Belsky, co-founder of Behance

Validate Your Idea

Once you have a start-up idea, it is crucial to validate it before investing considerable time and resources. Validation helps you ensure there is a demand for your product or service. Here is how to do it:

Build a Minimum Viable Product (MVP): Create a basic version of your product or service to evaluate with potential customers.

Get feedback: Collect feedback from early users to identify any shortcomings and make necessary improvements.

Conduct surveys and interviews: Reach out to your target audience to understand their needs and pain points.

Research the Competition: Study your competitors to see if there is a gap in the market that your start-up can fill.

Build a Team

Almost all successful start-ups were built by one or two people and then others would be brought in later. But my personal opinion is that a one to two people do not have the bandwidth to manage all the business processes that are involved, without help. Think about all these functions and how you would support them, I also noted what I did with CoreTactic:

- Marketing – I hired a firm.
- Finance – I hired a firm.
- Operations – This is us.
- Client Support – This is us.
- IT Support – I hired someone.
- Procurement – This is us.
- Legal – I hired someone.

Surround yourself with a talented team that complements your skills and shares your vision. Key team members may include co-founders, developers, marketers, and operations experts.

Marketing and Growth

Promoting your start-up is crucial for attracting customers and growing your business. Utilize various marketing strategies, including digital marketing, content marketing, social media, and networking.

Monitor and Adapt

Regularly analysis of key performance indicators (KPIs) to measure your start-up's success is critical to know what is broken and what is not. Be willing to adapt and pivot, if necessary, based on customer feedback and market changes.

Scale Your Business

As your start-up grows, consider scaling your operations. This may involve expanding your team, entering new markets, or diversifying your product offerings.

Launching a start-up is a challenging but rewarding endeavour. It requires a great idea, thorough planning, and relentless dedication. Contact CoreTactic today and I can help you launch your business.

Develop and Launch

With your idea validated, business plan in hand, and funding secured, it is time to develop your product or service and launch it into the market. Focus on delivering value to your customers and gathering data to refine your offering.

Remember that every successful start-up begins with a single step, so take that first step today, and embark on your entrepreneurial journey!

Finding FLOW?

When thinking about the type of business you would like to create, I challenge you to think back to a time when you worked on a project or some type of initiative, and completely lost track of time. When we are working on something, and I completely lose track of time it is called The Flow. When you are in The Flow, you are so focused on your work that everything else disappears into the background. Thank you to Mihaly Csikszentmihalyi, a world renown psychologist, for his research on motivational theory and the flow concept. Csikszentmihalyi challenged us with the questions "Who are you? What makes a good life? Is it money? An important job? Leisure time?" He believed our obsessive focus on such measures has led us astray. Work fills our days with anxiety and pressure, so that during our free time, I tend to live in boredom, absorbed by our screens.

If you can find work that will put you into the flow, then in my opinion you will find greater happiness in the work you do.

Handling Stress and Anxiety

Know thy self. For me personally, I already have a history of anxiety and depression, so I knew coming into a brand-new business venture would prove to be stressful, and I had to produce countermeasures at the beginning of the business to ensure that I did not burnout. The counter measures that I put in effect are very simple, 1st at 5:00 pm you're done work, walk away. You, your family, your friends, and your acquaintances are important in just about that order, if you can't take care of yourself then you cannot take care of your family, if you cannot take care of your family, then you cannot take care of your friends and colleagues, so know thyself. If you tend to be stressed or easily triggered by stress, make sure you produce a plan to prevent the stress from stressing you out! 😊

Starting a business can be stressful, and it is crucial to manage that stress. If you are too stressed or anxious, it can affect your body, your mind, and how well you work. You might feel tired, get annoyed easily, have trouble sleeping, get headaches, or have mood changes. All of this becomes a distraction and can lead to anxiety because you are not reaching your goals.

SO, it is important to find healthy ways to deal with these feelings. Activities like yoga, walking, dancing, or biking can help. They make you feel good and relax your mind. These activities are not just nice to have; they are important for keeping your stress down and help to make you feel positive.

Dealing with Imposter Syndrome

Sometimes, when you start a business, you might feel like you are not good enough or that you are pretending to be more skilled than you are. This is called imposter syndrome, and it is a common feeling among many people, no matter how educated or experienced you are, this can still affect you. Here is how you can overcome these doubts:

> **First, You Are Amazing:** Keep in mind that if you are reading this book and have a desire to start a business, you are not an idiot! Also, keep in mind that you are highly intelligent and can accomplish almost anything with focus, skill, and help. Just do not f#ck it up!
> **Celebrate Your Achievements**: Remember to give yourself credit for your successes. Celebrating small wins can boost your confidence.

Seek Feedback: Talk to others about your work. Getting positive and constructive feedback can help you see your true value.

Put Your Ego in Back Seat: Listening to and accepting feedback takes a certain amount of mindfulness and being vulnerable.

Affirm Your Strengths: Remind yourself of what you are good at. Recognize your skills and how they contribute to your success.

The Business Plan

Think of a business plan as your guide. It is a document that explains what your business is about, what you are planning to sell, who might buy your products or services, and how you expect to make money.

Writing this plan means you must really think about your business idea. This is the ideation phase. Here, you will produce ideas, research them, and make sure they are good enough to work in the real world. Another great reason to have a business plan is that you will have to formulate the way that you sell the business, so if you understand all aspects of your business, you will be a much better salesperson. Plus, if you are seeking a partner or someone to make a financial investment or maybe a loan for your start-up it is important to have a document to clearly articulate your vision and understand why you need the money.

The business plan for our start-up has the follow table of contents, and your plan will look similar:

> **Table of Contents**
>
> *The Mission*..................................
> *The Vision*...................................
> *How was < > Conceived?*...............
>   *Founders Background*..................
> *Our Services*................................
> *Values*..
> *Marketing Plan*............................
> *Sales Plan*...................................
> *Proposed Organizational Chart*......
> *Financial Backing*.........................

Writing a Comprehensive Business Plan

A good business plan is detailed and covers everything about your business. It should include:

Your Mission and Vision: What is the main goal of your business? What do you hope to achieve overall?

Do you know the difference between a mission and a vision? A mission is what you are planning to do with your business right now. A vision is where you want the world to be in the future, based on what your business can provide. So, for example, our mission is to provide unparalleled service to our clients and to help those in marginalized communities with support so that they can also be successful. And our vision is that someday, corporations will add more diversity to their workforce.

In addition to your business plan:

> **Product or Service Description**: Describe what you are selling or what service you are offering.
> **Market Analysis**: Who are your customers? Who are your competitors? What does the market look like?
> **Competitive Advantage**: What makes your business different or better than others?
> **Marketing Strategy**: How will you attract customers? How will you promote your business?
> **Operational Plan**: How will your business run day-to-day? Think about location, staff, and equipment.
> **Financial Plan**: This includes your budget, expected income, and expenses.
>
> *For a sample business plan template, see* https://www.coretactic.net/register-for-your-free-download/

Embrace Uncertainty

Starting a business comes with many unknowns. You will not have all the answers at the beginning, and that is okay. It is important to stay flexible and adapt as you learn more about your business and your customers.

Decide whether you are creating a new product or offering a service that already exists. This decision will influence many aspects of your business, like how you will price your products or services, how you will sell them, and what kind of legal requirements you will need to follow.

One of the initial steps in validating your business idea is to seek opinions from those around you. This involves having conversations with friends, family, and acquaintances, particularly those who either fall into your target customer category or possess expertise in your business field. The key here is to engage in meaningful dialogue that encourages honest and constructive feedback. It is crucial to approach this process with an open mind, prepared to hear a mix of positive and negative reactions. Another reminder to put your ego in to the back seat. It can be very humbling to receive feedback, always remember it is a gift.

Feedback, both complimentary and critical, serves as a crucial tool for refining your business concept. However, it is important to remember that not all feedback will be equally useful. When receiving input, consider the perspective and expertise of the individual providing it. Are they your target customers? Do they have experience in your industry? This will help you weigh the relevance and value of their opinions. Use this feedback not as a deterrent but to enhance and adapt your idea, ensuring it is resilient and market ready.

As you transition your business idea into a reality, addressing legal formalities is an essential step. For most entrepreneurs, navigating the legal landscape can be daunting. Engaging with a legal professional or utilizing reputable online legal services can provide guidance and clarity. These experts can assist in establishing the correct legal structure for your business and ensure compliance with relevant regulations and laws.

Chapter 2: Banks and Laws

Establishing a Business

First, hire a lawyer!

The process of legally establishing your business involves several key steps. These steps can vary significantly depending on the nature of your business. For instance, you may need to register your business name to protect your brand. Obtaining a business license is often necessary to operate legally, especially for certain industries like construction. For businesses that are set up as corporations, filing articles of incorporation is a mandatory requirement. Additionally, if you are entering a partnership, drafting a partnership agreement is crucial to outline the terms of the partnership. Each of these steps plays a vital role in laying a strong legal foundation for your business.

Securing Business Insurance

Insurance is a fundamental aspect of protecting your business from unforeseen events. A general business insurance policy typically provides coverage for various risks, including liability, property damage, and employee-related risks. The minimum coverage recommended is usually around $2 million, but this can vary depending on the specifics of your business. Factors such as the industry you operate in, the level of risk involved, and the scale of your operations will influence the amount of coverage you need. It is important to assess these factors carefully and choose a policy that adequately safeguards your business interests.

Additional Insurances

If your business plan includes paying yourself a salary or hiring employees, it is vital to secure worker's compensation insurance. This type of insurance is designed to cover medical expenses and lost wages for employees who might suffer work-related injuries or illnesses. It is not just a financial safety net for your employees; it also protects your business from potential legal complications arising from workplace incidents.

Obtaining Necessary Business Identifications

One of the first steps in establishing your business's financial and legal identity is to obtain an Employer Identification Number (EIN) from the Internal Revenue Service (IRS). This unique number is essential for your business as it is used for various tax-related purposes. It acts as a social security number for your business, allowing you to file taxes, open a bank account under your business name, and manage other official financial transactions.

Securing State Tax Identification

In addition to the EIN, your business will also require a state tax identification number. This is acquired from your state's department of revenue and is used specifically for managing state taxes. The state tax ID plays a crucial role, especially if your business will deal with sales tax, payroll tax, or other state-specific tax obligations. Each state has its own set of requirements and procedures for obtaining this number, so it is important to familiarize yourself with your specific state's regulations.

Setting Up Your Business Banking

Separating your personal and business finances is critical for maintaining clear financial records. Opening a business checking account dedicated solely to your business transactions is a step towards achieving this separation. Such an account will help you track your business income and expenses accurately, an essential aspect of fiscal management and tax reporting.

Establishing a Business Checking Account

Some things to consider when you are establishing a business checking account will be the amount of fees that you have to pay to maintain the account. For start-ups, some banks have a special program or product to help you that has lower limits and reduced fees. You will be excited to start your business, but you may not fully understand all the expense that you are incurring over time, so watch out for that!

Establishing a Business Credit Card

So, here is a trick question, when you are buying items and services for your business, can you use a personal credit card? If you answered yes, then you might be in trouble. It is highly recommended that you have a business credit card that is tied to your business. This is not only good financial practice, but your accountant will greatly appreciate it, especially if you have an audit coming up.

Establishing a High-Yield Savings Account

Alongside checking and credit accounts, setting up a high-yield savings account for your business can be a smart financial move. Allocating a portion of your profits to this account allows your money to grow through interest accrual. This liquid option is especially important, especially if you run out of cash for payroll or other larger expenses. Try to avoid credit cards as much as possible if you are low on funds. It may be better to take out a second mortgage on your private property to fund the business (make sure to discuss this with a financial expert). Then to rack up high interest debt. This not only aids in building an emergency fund but also provides a resource pool for future investments or unexpected expenses. It is a strategy that contributes to the financial health of your company.

In my past, a long time ago, I worked for a small start-up and was promoted to an executive role. Excited and could not wait to get started, then until I found out the company was in trouble; the bank was restricting funds. and my first question was "how much is in our emergency fund"? and was told "nothing."

As a side note, Health Insurance companies legally must have an emergency fund to cover all medical expenses for all customers over an X month period. Plus, start-ups fail almost hourly around the globe, show up one day and then disappear the next. Having an emergency stash of cash is critical.

Financial Planning for Your Business

Navigating the financial aspects of your business can be complex, especially if you are not well-versed in this area. Hiring an accountant can be a strategic move for entrepreneurs who need expertise in fiscal management. Accountants bring a wealth of knowledge in areas like bookkeeping, tax preparation, and financial reporting. They are instrumental in helping you manage your finances efficiently, saving you time and resources. Additionally, an accountant's expertise can prevent costly errors and penalties that can arise from mismanaged finances.

Budgeting and Cash Flow Management

One of the key areas where an accountant proves invaluable is in budget creation and cash flow forecasting. A well-planned budget provides a roadmap for your business's financial health, ensuring you allocate resources effectively. Cash flow forecasting, on the other hand, helps you anticipate and plan for future financial needs, enabling you to make informed decisions. An accountant's analytical skills are crucial in assessing your business's profitability and guiding you towards financial stability.

As your business grows and generates more revenue, diversifying your revenue streams becomes crucial for financial security. Investing in bonds and low-risk mutual funds is a prudent strategy to reduce reliance on a single income source. Diversification not only enhances your financial security but also contributes to the stability of your business eventually. It is a strategic approach to building a robust financial foundation that can withstand market fluctuations and economic changes.

By addressing these essential financial, legal, and personal well-being aspects, you are setting your business up for a successful launch. Having a comprehensive plan that covers these areas prepares you to face the diverse challenges and opportunities of your entrepreneurial journey. With a solid foundation, you will be better equipped to navigate the complexities of running a business and poised for sustainable growth and success.

WARNING: POTENTIAL SITUATION

When starting your business, it is extremely easy to get excited and sign up for many different software trials, systems that are online, and other tools that you think could be helpful. But then guess what happens? You forget about the trials and suddenly, a $1000 charge shows up on your credit card statement.

Lesson

When I was starting my business, I thought I would leverage AI to help me with materials, and research. So, I signed up for a paid version of ChatGPT. Little did I know that they only charge for an annual subscription, the full amount. $1000! ouch

Until you fully understand how your business is going to operate, try to hold off on buying too many different trials or software packages. Many software trials will come with a fee which needs to be paid after a certain time frame. And it is easy to be excited about your business and lose track of which trials you signed up for.

BLOG POST

Understanding the Legal Rights When Starting a Business

This article should not be used as legal advice. CoreTactic and/or Nick Rustad are not legal experts.

Starting a business is an exciting venture that involves creativity, innovation, and a passion for your chosen industry. However, amidst the enthusiasm, it is crucial to be well-versed in the legal aspects that come with entrepreneurship. This blog post aims to provide a comprehensive overview of the legal rights involved when embarking on the journey of starting a business.

Business Structure and Formation

One of the initial steps in starting a business is choosing its legal structure. Common options include sole proprietorship, partnership, limited liability company (LLC), and corporation. Each structure comes with its own set of legal implications, affecting factors such as liability, taxation, and management. Understanding the legal rights associated with your chosen structure is fundamental to the success of your business.

Intellectual Property Protection

Intellectual property (IP) is an asset for many businesses. Entrepreneurs must be aware of their legal rights to protect their innovations, brand identity, and creative works. Trademarks, patents, copyrights, and trade secrets are essential tools to safeguard intellectual property and prevent unauthorized use by competitors.

Contracts and Agreements

Contracts play a pivotal role in business operations. Whether dealing with customers, suppliers, employees, or partners, having well-drafted contracts is essential. Entrepreneurs have the legal right to negotiate and enter into agreements that protect their interests. Understanding contract law, including the elements of a valid contract and contractual obligations, is crucial for sound business transactions.

Employment Law and Labor Rights

Entrepreneurs must be aware of employment laws, including anti-discrimination regulations, minimum wage requirements, and workplace safety standards. Understanding and respecting the employment rights of employees is crucial to maintaining a compliant and ethical business.

One of the most effective ways to do this is by forming a Limited Liability Company (LLC). An LLC is a business structure that legally separates your personal assets from your business assets and liabilities. This separation is vital because it protects your personal possessions – like your home, car, or personal savings – in case your business faces legal issues or bankruptcy * According to LegalZoom, an online legal firm, a general rule, if the LLC cannot pay its debts, the LLC's creditors can go after the LLC's bank account and other assets. The owners' personal assets, such as cars, homes, and bank accounts, are safe. An LLC owner only risks the amount of money they have invested in business. *

Forming an LLC is not just about protection; it also offers other significant benefits. These include potential tax advantages, operational flexibility, and enhanced credibility with customers and suppliers. The tax benefits can be substantial, often allowing for more favourable tax treatments. Flexibility is another key advantage, as LLCs (Limited Liability Company) typically have less stringent requirements for reporting and governance compared to other business entities. This flexibility can be particularly beneficial for start-ups that are still finding their footing in the business world. Additionally, having an LLC adds a layer of professionalism and legitimacy to your business, which can be crucial in building trust and attracting clients. Another critical step in safeguarding your start-up is hiring a competent business lawyer. A lawyer specialized in business law can assist you with various legal aspects of your enterprise. This includes drafting contracts and agreements, navigating licenses and permits, and protecting intellectual property through trademarks and patents. Furthermore, a business lawyer plays a vital role in ensuring that your business complies with relevant laws and regulations, thereby reducing the risk of legal complications. They are also invaluable in resolving disputes that might arise with customers, suppliers, partners, employees, or competitors. Having a business lawyer can save you considerable time, money, and stress, while also decreasing your overall liability

Consumer Protection Laws

Entrepreneurs must comply with consumer protection laws to ensure fair and transparent business practices. Legal rights related to product warranties, advertising claims, and customer privacy must be upheld to build trust with consumers and avoid legal disputes.

Tax Obligations

Entrepreneurs are subject to various tax obligations, including income tax, sales tax, and payroll taxes. Knowing the legal rights and responsibilities related to taxation is vital to avoid legal issues and financial penalties. Consulting with a tax professional can help navigate the complexities of business taxation.

Environmental Compliance

Depending on the nature of the business, entrepreneurs may need to adhere to environmental regulations. Understanding and complying with these laws is essential to avoid legal repercussions and contribute to sustainable and responsible business practices.

In conclusion, starting a business involves navigating a complex legal landscape. Do not F it up! Entrepreneurs must be initiative-taking in understanding and exercising their legal rights to establish a solid foundation for their ventures. Seeking legal counsel and staying informed about evolving regulations are crucial steps in ensuring long-term success and compliance in the business world.

Chapter 3: start-up Death

No business in the history of business has started without at least one hiccup. It is OK to fail, but you want to make sure you understand why you failed and what you need to do differently the next time. If revenue is the problem, then a tip in this area, that could help you would be to run things in parallel. For example, try selling different services and using different e-mail formats and then see what the conversion rate is that you achieve. Conversion rate is the percentage of customers that go from a prospective customer to a paying customer. You may need to adjust based on how people perceive your message.

Statistics

You are not going to believe this, or maybe you will, but **90% of start-ups fail.** * (* see reference section in Appendix A) What the F!!! If so, with all the start-up failures, why do so many people try to make them work? The statistics above are according to HubSpot, a nice little (not so little) CRM platform. Starting a business is a journey filled with excitement and challenges. It is a path that many entrepreneurs embark on with high hopes and big dreams. However, the reality of starting a business is that it is fraught with risks and uncertainties. Many start-ups, despite seeming on the right track, can suddenly encounter failure. This stark reality is something I have seen firsthand among my colleagues. Some of their start-ups have not only failed but have also faced legal actions. It is a harsh reminder of the importance of safeguarding your venture.

The journey of a start-up is unpredictable. One moment, everything might appear to be progressing smoothly, and the next, you could be facing unforeseen challenges. These can range from financial difficulties, market competition, legal issues, to operational setbacks. The consequences of these challenges can be severe, leading to the ultimate downfall of the business. This sudden turn of events – from promise to peril – is what I refer to as 'start-up Death Cramps'. It is an abrupt halt to what might have seemed like a successful venture.

As stated previously, to avoid such disastrous outcomes, it is crucial to take steps to protect both yourself and your business. Hire a lawyer!

How to be a good boss

Another reason start-ups fail is due to poor leadership. It would do you a disservice, as my reader if I did not talk about leadership and how to be an effective and inspirational leader. If you are starting a business, you also need to build a healthy reputation with the people that collaborate with you, your business partners, and your customer base. If you want happy employees, you will want to listen to my advice and try it, if you do not give a s**t about people, you are going to have a tough time leading.

Being a good boss is extremely easy to do but there are key concepts that you need to practice being good at building your people and your team. The number one thing that I do when leading a team is jump in and help, I also keep asking "how can I help," because my job is not to be the big leader but to help the team! Do not forget, without your team you are nothing. One of my former leaders Rajiv gave this great advice, and I am grateful for my time on his team.

According to Daniel Pink's book Drive, people who tend to love their jobs and respect their boss also tend to have three things in common, can you guess what they are? Purpose, relatedness, and autonomy are the three. They have purpose, they have relatedness to what the business is achieving, and they have autonomy. Nothing can squash your leadership skills more than removing your team's purpose, relatedness, and autonomy. Being a good leader is also about getting to know your team and from my experience working in a corporation, every single person tends to have their guard up and they are not really showing their true authentic self. To be the best boss, you can and have your people fall in love with your leadership style, if you are vulnerable with them. Being vulnerable will help your team to be vulnerable with you which means they will develop more trust in your leadership. A team that trusts you will give more information to you that could be especially important. For example, if your team does not trust you, and someone makes a mistake that causes issues with the business, you may never know about it. The worst thing you can do is micromanage your team and build distrust. The potential result with be higher turnover, lower morale, and general disdain for the people they work with, and you.

I once had a horrible boss tell me that they did not have time to say "thank you" to their people. Asked them to share some "love" and say thank you to the team, because they were working so hard. They were one of the worst bosses I have ever had, ignorant, not loyal to their team and only cared about their reputation in the firm. Be available for your people, tell them thank you, and try to find little things that can make them happy and feel appreciated. We are all contributing to the company, let us build up and not down.

Understanding the Multifaceted Challenges of start-ups

Even with legal safeguards like forming an LLC and hiring a business lawyer, start-ups can still encounter various other challenges that can lead to failure. A study by CB Insights reveals some of the most common pitfalls that new businesses face.

In 2018 CB Insights conducted a study that investigated 111 start-ups that failed, and their findings were remarkably interesting. As you can see, cash, market, and competition are the most common causes of a start-up's failure.

The Pitfall of a Poorly Conceived Business Idea

A fundamental issue that many entrepreneurs encounter is falling too deeply in love with their own business idea without adequate market validation. There is a risk of not fully understanding the market's needs or overestimating the demand for the product or service. Entrepreneurs may also underestimate the complexities, costs, or time needed to bring their idea to fruition. To avoid this trap, it is essential to conduct thorough research, engage in rigorous testing, and seek honest feedback before launching. Flexibility is key; be prepared to pivot or modify your idea based on the insights you gather.

Funding: The Achilles' Heel of start-ups

Securing sufficient funding is a critical and ongoing challenge for start-ups. The sources of funding are diverse - personal savings, friends and family contributions, crowdfunding, angel investors, venture capitalists, loans, and grants, each with its advantages and disadvantages. Not all funding sources are suitable for every type of start-up. A realistic and comprehensive financial plan is vital. This plan should detail your start-up's income, expenses, cash flow, break-even point, and path to profitability. Equally important is a persuasive pitch that highlights your business's value proposition, market opportunity, competitive edge, existing traction, and growth prospects to attract potential investors or lenders.

Rescuing Your start-up

When facing challenges in your start-up, it can feel overwhelming. However, there are actionable strategies you can employ to navigate these difficulties and potentially save your business from failure.

Implementing Pro Bono Services

A valuable tactic to refine your product or service is to offer it for free or at a discounted rate for a brief period. This approach serves multiple purposes:

Testing and Validation: It allows you to evaluate your assumptions and validate the appeal of your product or service.

Feedback and Improvement: You receive direct feedback, which is crucial for making necessary adjustments.

Building Trust and Awareness: Offering free services or products can help build trust with potential customers and create word-of-mouth publicity.

Strategy for Conversion: While this approach can be beneficial, it is important to have a strategy for converting these customers into paying ones. It is also crucial to avoid devaluing your product or service and attracting only those interested in free offerings.

Leveraging Customer Feedback

Customer feedback is a goldmine of insights for any start-up:

Understanding Customer Needs: Feedback helps you understand what your customers like, what they do not, and what they expect from your product or service.

Identifying Business Strengths and Weaknesses: It provides a clear view of your business's strengths, weaknesses, opportunities, and threats.

Methodologies for Gathering Feedback: There are numerous ways to collect customer feedback – surveys, reviews, interviews, focus groups, and social media interactions are some of the effective methods.

Action on Feedback: The key is not just collecting feedback but acting on it. Show your customers how you have implemented their suggestions, and always express gratitude for their input.

Seeking Insights from Business Experts and Owners

Consulting with business experts or experienced business owners can offer new perspectives and valuable advice:

Gaining Expert Insights: These individuals can provide insights, tips, best practices, and resources that are invaluable for navigating business challenges.

Networking and Relationship Building: You can connect with experts through various channels – professional networks, online platforms, industry events, or business organizations.

Effective Communication: When seeking advice, be specific and clear about your needs. Respect their time and expertise and be open to constructive criticism.

Follow-Up and Gratitude: Keep them updated on your progress and how their advice has contributed to your business. This not only shows gratitude but also fosters ongoing relationships. Always remember to pay it forward, or backward. Help those who have helped you and those to come after you.

Navigating the challenges of a start-up requires a combination of strategic actions, openness to feedback, and a willingness to seek and apply expert advice. These strategies offer a pathway to refine your business model, strengthen customer relationships, and gain valuable insights, all of which are critical in steering your start-up away from potential failure and towards success.

Recognizing the Limits and Learning from Failure in start-ups

After implementing various strategies to overcome challenges in your start-up, you might witness a turnaround, transforming your venture into a success story. Yet, it is equally important to stay grounded and recognize when it may be time to discontinue your start-up.

Knowing When to Quit

In the entrepreneurial world, knowing when to quit can be as crucial as knowing how to succeed. If your start-up is continually struggling and shows no signs of viability or sustainability, it might be time to consider stepping back. This decision, though difficult, is sometimes necessary to avoid further losses and to preserve resources for future endeavours.

The Value of Failure

Failure, while often seen negatively, can be a powerful learning tool. Each failed venture provides insights and lessons that are invaluable for future projects. Embracing failure as part of the entrepreneurial journey allows you to grow and develop resilience. It is about extracting wisdom from setbacks and applying it to your next venture.

Leveraging Resources and Learning from Experts

Utilizing resources and learning from experts in the field can offer guidance and support in both success and failure scenarios. Here are some useful references:

CB Insights: offers insights into common reasons for start-up failures, which can help you avoid these pitfalls in the future.

Entrepreneur: highlights the benefits of hiring a business lawyer, emphasizing the importance of legal counsel in navigating business complexities.

Forbes: provides a comprehensive guide on forming an LLC, which is vital for legal protection and tax benefits.

Inc.: outlines several types of business insurance necessary to protect your start-up from potential risks and liabilities.

Small Business Administration: offers resources for writing a business plan, a crucial step in establishing a clear and structured path for your business.

As you navigate the challenges of running a start-up, remember that both success and failure offer opportunities for growth. By implementing strategic actions, seeking expert advice, and being realistic about your start-up's prospects, you are positioning yourself for long-term success in the entrepreneurial world. Whether your current venture succeeds or not, the experience and knowledge gained are invaluable assets for your future business endeavours.

As you work with your start-up, you may find yourself wanting to work within other industries. The following blog post addresses this, even though the blog post was for career work.

BLOG POST

Navigating Career Transitions: Key Considerations for Switching Industries

Embarking on a career change can be a daunting but rewarding journey. Whether you are feeling unfulfilled in your current role, seeking new challenges, or pursuing a long-held passion, transitioning to a different industry requires careful planning and consideration. In this blog post, we will explore essential factors to contemplate when contemplating a career change.

Self-Reflection

Before diving into a new industry, take the time for honest self-reflection. Assess your skills, strengths, and weaknesses. Consider your values, interests, and long-term career goals. Understanding your motivations for wanting a change will help guide your decisions and ensure alignment with your personal and professional aspirations.

Research

Thoroughly research the industry in which you are interested. Gain insights into its current trends, job market stability, and growth potential. Explore the required skills and qualifications for positions within the new field. Networking with professionals in the industry can provide valuable firsthand information and perspectives.

Skill Assessment

Identify the transferable skills you possess that can be applied to the new industry. Consider pursuing additional education or certifications to fill any skill gaps. Many industries value adaptable skills such as communication, problem-solving, and project management, which can be assets in almost any field.

Financial Preparedness

A career change may come with a temporary fiscal impact. Assess your current financial situation, including savings and potential changes in income. Consider creating a financial buffer to ease the transition period. It is also wise to research average salaries in the new industry to set realistic expectations.

Networking

Building a strong professional network is crucial when changing industries. Attend industry events, join online forums, and connect with professionals on platforms like LinkedIn. Networking can open doors to potential mentors, job opportunities, and valuable insights that can facilitate a smoother transition.

Evaluate the Waters

Before committing fully to a new career path, explore it on a smaller scale. Consider taking on freelance projects, volunteering, or pursuing internships in the new industry. This firsthand experience will provide valuable insights and confirm whether the industry is the right fit for you.

Update Your Brand

Revise your resume, LinkedIn profile, and other professional materials to highlight the transferable skills and experiences relevant to the new industry. Tailor your application materials to showcase your enthusiasm and commitment to making the transition.

Seek Guidance

Consider seeking guidance from career counsellors, mentors, or industry professionals who have successfully navigated similar transitions. Their advice and insights can be invaluable in providing direction and support throughout the process.

Changing careers is a major decision that requires careful consideration and planning. By engaging in self-reflection, conducting thorough research, assessing your skills, preparing financially, networking, gaining firsthand experience, updating your professional brand, and seeking guidance, you can navigate a successful transition into a new industry. This type of change is difficult, but not impossible, especially if you work with CoreTactic to make it happen! Remember, a well-thought-out strategy and an initiative-taking approach can turn a career change into a fulfilling and enriching experience.

Chapter 4: start-up Re-birth

"There's nothing wrong with staying small. You can do big things with a small team." — Jason Fried, CEO of Basecamp

Failure or Re-birth

After overcoming significant challenges, you are at a pivotal point to relaunch your business. A critical aspect of this relaunch is ensuring you have a robust and efficient CRM (customer relationship management) platform that includes a payment collection system. This system is not just a tool for transactions; it is a cornerstone for customer satisfaction and financial stability.

With CoreTactic, I started by doing it ALL. Initially, I wanted to have life, career, business, and executive coaches, plus internet reputation search and repair, resumes, cover letters, and LinkedIn profile services. BUT it was too much. Plus, I was authoring this book, and trying to raise funds for a foundation. The CoreTactic Foundation will be designed to help curb homelessness, by offering free coaching services to low-income people who are on the edge of losing it all.

Go Back to Basics

So, for our first re-birth, I decided to drop the business and life coaching services and focus on career and executive coaching only. Will still have life and business coaches on staff, if the need should arise, but I want to focus on a core offering. Also, I am also no longer providing internet reputation repair, and our foundation is on hold for a little bit. Overall revenue for the first 4 months (September-December 2023), was around $4-5K per month, then in January of 2024 it dropped to $2K, it was at this point that I needed to do something. By removing extra services and changing our rate structure, I have witnessed a positive impact on the business.

Payment Collection System

Ensuring timely and complete payments for your products or services is also critical. A reliable payment collection system helps avoid potential disputes or issues with customers, contributing to a smooth business operation. It is not just about receiving payments; it is about creating a seamless and trustworthy transaction process for your customers.

The digital age offers a variety of online payment collection tools, each with unique features and benefits. Popular choices include Square, Stripe, PayPal, and Shopify. These platforms cater to different business models and sizes. The choice of a payment system should align with your specific business needs and customer preferences.

Ease of Use

The system should be straightforward to set up and manage. It should offer a user-friendly interface for both you and your customers. A clear checkout process and reliable customer support are essential for a smooth operation. The easier it is to navigate, the more likely your customers will complete their purchases without issues.

Security

In an era where data breaches are common, choosing a payment system that adheres to high-security standards like PCI, DSS, GDPR, or CCPA is vital. It should safeguard both your and your customers' data and privacy. Features that prevent fraud and provide efficient dispute resolution are essential components of a secure payment system.

Cost

Transparency in pricing is critical. Choose a system with clear, upfront costs, avoiding hidden fees. Competitive rates, flexible plans, and low transaction fees can significantly impact your profitability. A cost-effective system is crucial, especially for start-ups that need to manage resources judiciously.

Integration

The system should seamlessly integrate with your existing website, platform, or software. It should support various payment methods – credit cards, debit cards, e-wallets, bank transfers – catering to a broader customer base. Additionally, it should easily integrate with other tools and services you use, such as accounting software, invoicing systems, or Customer Relationship Management (CRM) tools, to streamline your business processes.

As you relaunch your start-up, selecting the right payment collection system is more than a logistical decision; it is a strategic one that impacts customer experience and operational efficiency. The chosen system should be easy to use, secure, cost-effective, and integrally compatible with your existing business processes. This choice is a critical step in building a solid foundation for your relaunched business, ensuring you're well-equipped to handle transactions smoothly and professionally.

WARNING: POTENTIAL SITUATION

It is impossible to know what will be successful when you start a business. At the very beginning, and as you build your processes you will inevitably pick up tools and systems that do not meet your needs, it will take time for you to discover that is the case. At CoreTactic, I had a remarkably interesting beginning. When I formed the company in 2022, and with my technology background, I was able to set up a SharePoint site, billing system, website, and a variety of other tools. But while I were thinking about our re-birth, I also discovered that our processes were so desegregated. Needed a tool that could combine everything into one experience from paying for a service, scheduling a meeting, and keeping notes on each client's needs so that I can continue to help them for years. A unified solution was needed, because I could not track each client, at a particular stage in the sales or delivery steps. It is particularly important to know where your customers are from their interactions with you, and in your sales pipeline.

You will want to address your customers differently if they are a prospective verse a paying customer. Some companies will focus all their customer service prowess on the new customers coming in and provide less quality customer service to existing customers. Thus, focusing on new business. Some companies do the opposite.

In the context of relaunching your start-up, integrating a good payment collection system can significantly impact various aspects of your business. Below are some of the key benefits such a system can provide:

Ease and Speed of Transactions

A streamlined payment system simplifies the process for customers to complete their purchases, making it quicker and more convenient.

Multiple Payment Options

Offering a variety of payment methods caters to a broader range of customer preferences, potentially increasing the likelihood of sales.

Enhancing Cash Flow and Financial Management
Efficiency in Payment Collection

A robust system reduces the time and effort required to process payments, thereby improving the efficiency of your cash flow.

Access to Real-time Financial Data

Modern payment systems often provide real-time analytics and reports, giving you valuable insights into your financial status and helping you make informed business decisions.

Increasing Satisfaction and Trust
Smooth and Secure Payment Experience

A reliable payment system that ensures a secure and hassle-free payment experience enhances customer trust and satisfaction.

Effective Dispute Resolution

The ability to manage any payment issues or disputes further strengthens customer confidence quickly and professionally in your business.

BLOG POST

A Guide to Setting and Achieving Daily Goals

At CoreTactic, I believe that setting and achieving your daily goals is critical to success. When faced with a massive objective, break it down to daily goals and you will feel so much more successful!

In the hustle and bustle of our daily lives, it is easy to get caught up in the chaos and lose sight of our long-term objectives. This is where the power of setting and achieving daily goals comes into play. Whether you are striving for personal development, career advancement, or simply looking to make the most of your day, a structured approach to daily goal setting can work wonders. In this blog post, we will provide you with a comprehensive guide on how to set and achieve your daily goals effectively.

STEP 1: REFLECT AND PRIORITIZE

Before diving into goal setting, take a moment to reflect on your long-term aspirations. What are the bigger objectives you want to achieve? By aligning your daily goals with these larger ambitions, you will create a sense of purpose and motivation.

Once you have an unobstructed vision, prioritize your goals. Not all tasks are created equal, so focus on those that will have the most significant impact on your life or work.

STEP 2: SMART GOALS

SMART is an acronym that stands for Specific, Measurable, Achievable, Relevant, and Time-bound. Your daily goals should meet these criteria:

Specific: Define your goal with precision. Avoid vague objectives like "be more productive" and opt for something like "complete a draft of the report."

Measurable: Determine how you will measure your progress and success. For instance, "write 1,000 words of the novel."

Achievable: Ensure your goal is realistic and attainable. Setting overly ambitious goals can lead to frustration.

Relevant: Your daily goals should be aligned with your long-term goals, as mentioned in Step 1.

Time-bound: Set a deadline for each goal. This creates a sense of urgency and helps you manage your time effectively.

STEP 3: BREAK GOALS INTO TASKS

Once you have defined your daily goals, break them down into smaller tasks or steps. This makes them more manageable and less overwhelming. For example, if your goal is to "complete a draft of the report," tasks might include "research, outline, write introduction," and so on.

STEP 4: CREATE A DAILY SCHEDULE

Incorporate your goal-related tasks into your daily schedule. Use time management techniques such as time blocking to allocate specific time slots for each task. Be realistic about how much you can accomplish in a day to avoid overloading yourself.

STEP 5: STAY ACCOUNTABLE

Accountability is key to achieving daily goals. Share your goals with a friend, family member, or colleague who can help keep you on track. Alternatively, consider using a journal or task management app to monitor your progress.

STEP 6: REVIEW AND ADJUST

At the end of the day, review your progress. Celebrate your achievements and identify any areas where you fell short. Use this information to adjust your goals and approach as needed. Flexibility is crucial to adapt to unforeseen circumstances.

Setting and achieving daily goals is a powerful strategy for personal growth and productivity. By following this guide and integrating goal setting into your daily routine, you will find yourself making steady progress toward your larger life objectives. Remember, success is not just about reaching the destination; it is also about enjoying the journey and the small victories along the way. So, go ahead, set those daily goals, and watch as they propel you toward a more fulfilling life.

Chapter 5: Start Cooking

Congratulations! You have earned either one of two congratulations, congratulations you are now homeless and have spent all your money OR congratulations you are starting to make some money. With any start-up things can easily go in either direction.

Compliance

Now that your business is moving, let us make sure you do not get into trouble. Compliance-related risks are a significant challenge for start-ups, and they can lead to regulatory fines, data breaches, and loss of customer trust. According to a recent study, regulatory and legal hurdles rank as the fifth leading cause of start-up failures, closely trailing behind the fierce competition in the market. *

*Note: * denotes more information and references in Appendix B.*

To overcome this, start-ups need to consider compliance not as a burdensome chore but rather think of it as a strategic advantage that pushes their start-up ahead. *

Start-ups are subject to various regulatory obligations, and compliance management is necessary to ensure that they operate within the boundaries of the law and mitigate potential penalties. * Customers also want their start-up vendors to have a solid security framework before collaborating with them and entrusting their data. * Therefore, it is essential to choose the right compliance framework that focuses on different considerations. *

Here are a couple compliance risks that start-ups need to know about:

Failure to incorporate correctly: When establishing your tech start-up, it is crucial to get your incorporation right.

Permanent establishment risk: Many tech start-ups work across borders, opening them up to permanent establishment risk.

Invalid or absent employee agreements: Employee agreements are essential to protect your start-up's intellectual property and confidential information.

Misclassifying employees and contractors: Misclassifying employees and contractors can lead to significant legal and financial consequences.

You have reached a significant milestone in your business journey where your enterprise is now generating steady income and experiencing growth. While this achievement is commendable, it also brings forth new challenges and responsibilities. In this chapter, I will delve into key aspects you must consider when managing and scaling your business. These include budgeting, taxation, documentation, and customer retention.

Budgeting for Success

One of the fundamental pillars of running a thriving business is the establishment of a realistic and effective budget. A budget serves as a strategic plan that outlines your anticipated income and expenses over a specified period, whether it is monthly, quarterly, or annually.

Creating and adhering to a well-structured budget offers several advantages:

Advantages of Budgeting
Financial Tracking and Progress

A budget allows you to closely monitor your financial performance and track your progress toward your financial goals.

Cost Control

It empowers you to identify and control costs and expenditures, ensuring that your business operates efficiently.

Resource Allocation

Budgets help in allocating resources effectively, enabling you to prioritize essential activities and investments.

Future Planning

By forecasting income and expenses, budgets enable you to plan and anticipate potential challenges or opportunities.

Informed Decision-Making

With a budget in place, you can make informed and strategic decisions aligned with your financial objectives.

Creating a Budget

To establish an effective budget, you should follow these steps:

Estimate Your Income: Determine the expected income from your products, services, and any other revenue sources, such as grants or donations. Use historical sales data, market research, and industry benchmarks to project income. Consider seasonal or cyclical fluctuations and be conservative in your estimates.

Estimate Your Expenses: Calculate the expected expenses for your business operations, covering areas like rent, utilities, salaries, supplies, marketing, taxes, and more. Rely on past expense records, vendor quotes, or industry standards for expense estimation. Account for both fixed and variable costs and maintain realistic estimations.

Calculate Profit or Loss: The difference between income and expenses defines your profit or loss. If income exceeds expenses, you have a profit; if expenses exceed income, you incur a loss. Use the simple formula: Profit or Loss = Income - Expenses.

Regular Budget Review and Adjustment: Continuously monitor your budget, comparing it with actual income and expenses. This practice allows you to track financial performance and identify any discrepancies. Be prepared to adjust the budget in response to changing circumstances, new opportunities, or unexpected events.

WARNING: POTENTIAL SITUATION

Having a budget is great, but following a budget is even better. Find someone who can hold you accountable and ensure you are sticking to the budget.

Budgeting is a dynamic process that plays a pivotal role in your business's financial stability and growth. It helps you maintain financial discipline, allocate resources judiciously, and make well-informed decisions to steer your business toward continued success.

Additional benefits of having a good budget are:

> **Increased profitability:** A good budget can help you increase your profitability by maximizing your income and minimizing your expenses. It can also help you optimize your pricing, improve your cash flow, and invest in your growth.
>
> **Reduced risk:** A good budget can help you reduce your risk by preparing you for any financial challenges or uncertainties. It can also help you avoid overspending, under-pricing, or running out of cash.

Enhanced accountability: A good budget can help you enhance your accountability by setting clear and measurable financial goals and targets. It can also help you track and evaluate your performance and progress and hold yourself and your team responsible for the results.

Taxation

Another important aspect of running a successful business is to comply with the relevant tax laws and regulations. Taxes are mandatory payments that you must make to the government, based on your income, sales, or other factors. Taxes can vary depending on your business type, location, industry, and size. Some of the common types of taxes that you may have to pay are:

Income tax: This is the tax that you must pay on your net income, which is your income minus your expenses. The income tax rate and filing requirements depend on your business structure, such as sole proprietorship, partnership, corporation, or LLC. You may also have to pay estimated taxes, which are quarterly payments that you make throughout the year, based on your projected income and expenses.

Sales tax: This is the tax you must collect and remit to the government, based on sales of your products or services. The sales tax rate and rules depend on your location, industry, and product or service type. You may also have to register for a sales tax permit, file sales tax returns, and keep records of your sales and tax payments.

Payroll tax: This is the tax you must withhold and pay to the government, based on the wages and salaries you pay your employees. The payroll tax consists of two parts: the employer's portion and the employee's portion. The employer's portion includes Social Security tax, Medicare tax, and unemployment tax. The employee's portion includes federal income tax, state income tax, and local income tax. You may also have to file payroll tax returns, issue W-2 forms, and keep records of your payroll and tax payments.

To manage your taxes, you need to:
Understand your tax obligations!

You need to research and understand the tax laws and regulations that apply to your business, and how they affect your income, expenses, sales, and payroll. You can use online resources, such as the IRS website, the SBA website, or your state and local tax authorities' websites, to learn more about your tax obligations. I strongly recommend that you work with a tax professional, such as an accountant or a lawyer, for expert advice and guidance.

Plan and prepare your taxes.

You need to plan and prepare your taxes ahead of time and avoid any last-minute surprises or errors. You can use online tools, such as QuickBooks, TurboTax, or FreshBooks, to help you organize and track your income, expenses, sales, and payroll, and to calculate and file your taxes. You can also use online calculators, such as the IRS Withholding Calculator, the Sales Tax Calculator, or the Payroll Tax Calculator, to help you estimate your tax payments and deductions.

Pay and file your taxes.

You need to pay and file your taxes on time and in full and avoid any penalties or interest. You can use online methods, such as the IRS Direct Pay, the Electronic Federal Tax Payment System, or the Electronic Funds Withdrawal, to pay your taxes electronically. You can also use online methods, such as the IRS Free File, the IRS e-file, or the IRS Online Services, to file your tax returns electronically.

Some of the benefits of managing your taxes well are:

> **Reduced tax liability:** Managing your taxes well can help you reduce your tax liability by taking advantage of tax deductions, credits, exemptions, or incentives for which you may qualify. These can help you lower your taxable income, increase your tax refund, or decrease your tax payment.
> **Avoided tax problems:** Managing your taxes well can help you avoid tax problems, such as audits, notices, penalties, or interest, which can result from late, incomplete, or incorrect

tax payments or filings. These can cause you stress, hassle, and extra costs, and damage your reputation or credibility.

Improved tax planning: Managing your taxes well can help you improve your tax planning, which is the process of analysing and optimizing your financial situation and goals in relation to your taxes. This can help you make better financial decisions, such as choosing the best business structure, investing in your growth, or saving for retirement.

Documentation Requirements

Another important aspect of running a successful business is to have proper and accurate documentation. Documentation is the process of creating and maintaining records of your business activities, transactions, and information. Documentation can include distinct types of documents, such as contracts, invoices, receipts, reports, policies, procedures, manuals, and more. Documentation can help you:

Comply with legal and regulatory requirements: Documentation can help you comply with the legal and regulatory requirements that apply to your business, such as tax laws, labor laws, privacy laws, or industry standards. Documentation can also help you prove your compliance in case of any disputes, audits, or investigations.

Manage your business operations: Documentation can help you manage your business operations, such as accounting, finance, marketing, sales, human resources, or customer service. Documentation can also help you monitor and measure your performance and progress and identify and resolve any issues or problems.

Communicate and collaborate with others: Documentation can help you communicate and collaborate with others, such as your customers, suppliers, partners, employees, or investors. Documentation can also help you establish and maintain trust, transparency, and accountability with your stakeholders.

To create and maintain documentation, you need to:

Define your documentation needs: You need to define your documentation needs, based on your business type, size, industry, and goals. You need to determine what types of documents you need to create and keep, how often you need to update them, and how long you need to retain them. You also need to consider the format, style, and tone of your documents, and the audience and purpose of your documents.

Use documentation tools and systems: You need to use documentation tools and systems, such as Microsoft Word, Google Docs, Dropbox, or Evernote, to help you create, store,

Chapter 6: Sustainability

"Sustainable development is the development that meets the needs of the present without compromising the ability of future generations to meet their own needs." – Gro Harlem Brundtland, former prime minister of Norway and chair of the World Commission on Environment and Development.

Sustainability, in the context of a start-up, transcends mere longevity—it embodies a commitment to maintaining or enhancing the quality and performance of your enterprise. In addition, while mitigating negative impacts on the environment, society, and the economy at large. It is not merely an ethical obligation; rather, it serves as a strategic advantage that can set your business apart in an increasingly conscientious world.

In this chapter, I delve into the crucial concept of sustainability and its pivotal component—diversification, which I wrote about earlier regarding revenue stream diversification. Sustainability serves as the bedrock upon which you can build a business that stands the test of time. By strategically diversifying your offerings, you can reduce dependence on singular factors, thereby safeguarding your business against market downturns, logistical issues, and other challenges that may jeopardize your operations.

Diversification

The advantages of diversification are multifaceted. It not only fortifies your business against unforeseen challenges but also positions you to provide enhanced value, choice, and convenience to your clients. Moreover, diversification opens doors to new niches, segments, or regions, sharpening your competitive edge.

Next, I will explore various facets of diversification within your business. Our aim is to equip you with the knowledge and strategies needed to implement diversification effectively. Will delve into product or service diversification, market diversification, and income diversification. Off insights, examples, and real-life cases that illustrate how these strategies can be applied in the context of your business.

By the end of this chapter, you will have a comprehensive understanding of how sustainability and diversification can work hand in hand to ensure the longevity, resilience, and success of your business. Moreover, you will gain practical insights into implementing diversification strategies that align with your start-up niche and objectives. With the right approach, your business can not only thrive but also contribute positively to the world around it.

Market Diversification

Market diversification involves the strategic expansion of your business into new markets or segments, with the aim of reaching a broader and more diverse audience. This diversification strategy allows you to tap into previously untapped customer bases and extend your services to a wider range of clients.

Examples of Market Diversification
Targeting Different Customer Types

To diversify your market, consider offering your business services to various customer types. This could include individuals seeking personal development, working with organizations to enhance employee performance, or providing specialized coaching to specific groups or communities. At CoreTactic, I have advertisements, or participate in a wide and diverse segment of the population through Groupon, fiverr, UpWork, Craigslist, and a variety of other sites.

Focusing on Diverse Demographics and Geographics

Another way to diversify your market is by tailoring your business to different demographics and geographics. You can target clients of various ages, genders, income levels, lifestyles, locations, or cultural backgrounds. This expansion broadens your reach and relevance.

Exploring Various Promotion and Delivery Channels

To successfully diversify your market, explore different channels and platforms for promoting and delivering your coaching services. Utilize social media platforms, start a podcast to reach a wider audience, or consider using newsletters and other online tools to connect with your target market.

Income Diversification

Income diversification is the strategy of creating multiple income sources that complement your core business income. This approach helps increase your financial stability and security by reducing your reliance on a single income stream.

Examples of Income Diversification

Offering Different Pricing and Payment Options: To diversify your income, provide clients with various pricing and payment options. This may include hourly rates for individual sessions, predefined packages for extended engagements, subscription-based models, membership programs, or even donation-based pricing for added flexibility.

Creating Passive Income Streams: Passive income streams can significantly bolster your income diversification efforts. Explore opportunities such as affiliate marketing, where you promote products or services related to your niche and earn commissions on sales. Additionally, consider advertising on your platform or website to generate passive income.

Collaborating and Partnering with Other Professionals: Collaboration is a powerful income diversification strategy. Partnering with other professionals, or organizations can open new income streams. Collaborations can lead to referrals, shared opportunities, joint ventures, and cost-sharing arrangements, all of which contribute to diversified income sources. A great friend and business associate in a third party that offers career assessments to our clients. Added an additional service to sell and did so without additional up-front cost.

Product or Service Diversification

Imagine your products and/or services are listed on a menu in a restaurant. You can keep serving the same dishes, but adding new ones or tweaking the recipes can make your restaurant a hot spot. Similarly, diversifying your products and services can spice up your business. Another idea is to let your customers mix and match to create a completely unique and custom solution. Here is how you can do it:

Expand Your Services

Offer diverse types of services to cater to various client needs. As an example, with our business, providing coaching services, you could provide life coaching, executive coaching, business coaching, health and wellness coaching, or any other specialized coaching that aligns with your expertise. This would be instead of only providing one service.

Explore Different Formats

Consider offering your services and products in various formats, such as online courses, webinars, podcasts, books, or mobile apps. This allows clients to choose what suits them best, expanding your reach.

In addition, not only can you create products and services of various formats, but you can also create different price points. For example, we have been working with an online tool to find clients called Fiverr. With Fiverr it is possible to set up the types of services and prices you can offer your clients. For example, I have a bronze package on Fiverr that offers 2 hours of coaching and a new resume for $200.00, but I also have silver and gold options which provide more coaching time along with additional services. A variety of options and prices are best to ensure you can be open to any type of customer. Then, you may want to trim it back. So not only do you want to explore different formats and variations for your customer base, but you also want to have different price points because socioeconomically you are going to want to market to a wide range of customers.

Create Products

Develop tools, resources, or merchandise that complement your services. These could include assessments, worksheets, planners, journals, or branded merchandise like apparel.

Chapter 7: Sourcing Client Leads

"In sales, you don't have to be better than your competition, you just have to be different." - Bill Gates

One of the most important components of running a successful business is to have a steady and consistent flow of qualified leads, who are potential clients that are interested in and ready for your services.

However, finding and attracting these leads can be challenging, especially in a competitive and saturated market. That is why you need to have a strategic and effective lead generation plan, which can help you reach and connect with your ideal customers and convert them into loyal and satisfied clients.

When I started our business, I only found two avenues for sourcing clients. The first was LinkedIn, which is a professional social networking platform, where I could create and optimize our profile, showcase our expertise and credentials, and build relationships with our target audience.

The second was Bark, which is an online marketplace, where I could register and list our services, and receive inquiries and requests from potential clients who were looking for coaches. In our opinion, LinkedIn is the best option for us, since Bark is a little too expensive for a start-up. Working with LinkedIn, without any of their add-ins or tools, was free. When working with Bark, there was a cost per lead, and the cost was variable depending on the client situation, their age, their experience, their location, and what services they needed.

However, I did not feel good about only having two sources or channels to source clients, because I did not like the restriction. If the LinkedIn website or Bark went offline for a day, it could have a significant impact on our revenue. Moreover, I wanted to expand our reach and exposure, and diversify our income streams.

So, over the course of a couple of months, I investigated other lead sources, and I have found several more that I can tap into, plus some tools that could be helpful. Here are some of the lead sources and tools that I have discovered and implemented:

Search Engine Optimization (SEO)

This is a big one! I thought SEO was a strange and complicated topic, but it is not. Basically, SEO helps search engines catalogue your website effectively. If you follow SEO best practices, then you will see an increase in website traffic.

This is the process of improving the visibility and ranking of our website on search engines, such as Google or Bing, by optimizing our content, keywords, links, and technical aspects. SEO can help us attract organic and relevant traffic to our website, where I can showcase our services, testimonials, and credentials, and capture leads through opt-in forms, landing pages, or calls to action. SEO can also help us establish our authority and credibility, by providing valuable and informative content, such as blog posts, articles, videos, or podcasts that answer our audience's questions, problems, or goals.

Email Marketing

Email marketing is a powerful tool for fostering meaningful connections with your leads and clients. This process involves using email as a means of communication to engage with your audience by delivering personalized and relevant messages. These messages can take various forms, including newsletters, special offers, promotions, or follow-up messages. Email marketing serves as a dynamic platform for nurturing relationships, building trust, and encouraging action.

Nurturing Leads and Building Trust

One of the primary roles of email marketing is nurturing leads and establishing trust and rapport. This is achieved by delivering valuable and informative content directly to your audience's inbox. At CoreTactic, I use many methods to build leads and trust. First, your business must have credentialed resources. For example, if you are running a coaching business, then you should have people who are trained and certified in coaching. Second, I formed partnerships with strong organizations to show CoreTactic is legitimate, and as an influencing tactic (everyone is doing it). Vetted numerous times.

Through emails, you can provide your leads with a wealth of resources, such as practical tips, expert advice, engaging stories, or compelling case studies. This content not only highlights your expertise but also demonstrates tangible results, further solidifying your credibility.

Converting and Retaining Clients

Beyond nurturing leads, email marketing plays a pivotal role in converting leads into clients and maintaining lasting relationships. It prompts your audience to take specific actions that align with your services. These actions may include scheduling a discovery call to explore your offerings, enrolling in a business program, or contributing through reviews and referrals.

The power of email marketing lies in its ability to engage your audience with personalized and relevant messages. By tailoring your content to their interests, needs, and preferences, you can increase the likelihood of conversions and client retention. The continuous communication facilitated by email marketing keeps your brand at the forefront of your audience's minds, making it more likely they will turn to you when seeking business services or solutions.

Email marketing is not just a communication channel; it is a relationship-building tool. It allows you to reach out to your audience in a personalized and meaningful way, creating a sense of connection and community. As I explore the intricacies of email marketing in the following sections, you will discover strategies to optimize your campaigns, craft compelling messages, and leverage this platform to its fullest potential.

WARNING: POTENTIAL SITUATION

Recommendation is to find a platform where you can send mass emails that can temper the distribution, so that you do not set off any spam alerts.

Story

Worked at start-up company that used mass e-mail marketing and they were flagged as spam and their domain name was prevented from sending e-mail. You do not want to make marketing harder than it already is, so please be careful.

Lesson

Be careful with email marketing, too much, and you could be shut off. All email providers want to maintain their reputation, and if they support spam, it could hurt their business.

Through effective email marketing, you can build stronger connections, foster trust, and drive conversions, achieving your business goals and objectives.

Online Advertising

This is the process of using paid methods to promote and advertise our services, on various online platforms, such as search engines, social media, websites, or apps. Online advertising can help us reach and target our ideal customers, by using specific criteria, such as keywords, demographics, interests, or behaviours, to display our ads to them. Online advertising can also help us generate and measure our leads, by using tracking and analytics tools, such as Google Ads, Facebook Ads, or Instagram Ads, to monitor and optimize our campaigns.

Social Media

When you start to get a little older (+45) social media may become more of a pain than a benefit. Personally, for me, that is the case and why I hired a marketing firm to manage this aspect.

This is the process of using social media platforms, such as Facebook, Twitter, Instagram, or YouTube, to create and share content. Content will be posts, stories, images, or videos, which showcase our business, personality, values, and vision. It is important to interact and engage with our audience, such as likes, comments, shares, and messages.

Social media can help us increase our brand awareness and recognition, by reaching and attracting a large and diverse audience, and by creating a loyal and supportive community. Social media can also help us generate and qualify our leads, by using features and tools, such as polls, quizzes, live streams, or chatbots, to collect feedback, information, or contact details from our audience.

Networking

This is the process of connecting and building relationships with other people, such as partners, professionals, or organizations, who share similar or complementary interests, goals, or values, and who can provide you with referrals, leads, or opportunities.

Networking can help us expand our reach and exposure, by accessing and tapping into other people's networks, and by creating a positive and memorable impression. Networking can also help us enhance our reputation and credibility, by establishing and maintaining trust, reciprocity, and collaboration with other people.

These are some of the lead sources and tools that I have discovered and implemented, and they have helped us grow our business and client base. By using a combination of these strategies, I have been able to create a diversified and sustainable lead generation plan that can help us reach and connect with our ideal customers and convert them into loyal and satisfied clients.

BLOG POST

The Power of Networking: Your Pathway to Finding Your Dream Job

In today's competitive job market, finding the perfect job can be a daunting task. With countless resumes flooding employers' inboxes, you might wonder how to stand out from the crowd. The answer lies in the age-old practice of networking. Building and nurturing professional relationships can be your secret weapon in securing that dream job. In this blog post, we will delve into the value of networking with people and how it can significantly enhance your job search.

Expanding Your Horizons

Networking opens doors to a world of opportunities you might not have encountered otherwise. When you engage with people from diverse backgrounds, industries, and experiences, you gain access to a wealth of knowledge and perspectives. These insights can help you identify the career path that truly resonates with you, leading you toward a job that aligns with your passions and skills.

Learning from Others

Networking is not just about finding job leads; it is about learning from others. By connecting with professionals who have walked similar career paths, you can gain valuable insights, advice, and tips. Learning from their successes and setbacks can help you navigate your own career journey more effectively.

Job Referrals and Recommendations

One of the most tangible benefits of networking is the potential for job referrals and recommendations. When you have built a strong network, people are more likely to vouch for your skills and work ethic. Many jobs are never even advertised publicly because employers prefer to hire through referrals, making your network a crucial source of job opportunities.

Staying Informed

In today's fast-paced job market, staying informed about industry trends and job openings is essential. Networking can help you stay updated on the latest developments, allowing you to position yourself as a valuable candidate. Joining relevant industry groups, attending conferences, and following industry leaders on social media can provide you with the inside scoop on job openings and emerging opportunities.

Building Confidence

Networking can boost your confidence, which is a critical asset in the job search process. Engaging in meaningful conversations with professionals in your field can help you refine your elevator pitch, improve your communication skills, and gain self-assurance in your abilities. This newfound confidence will shine through when you are interviewing for your dream job.

Fostering Long-Term Relationships

Effective networking is not just about what others can do for you; it is also about what you can do for them. Building mutually beneficial relationships can lead to long-term professional connections. By offering your expertise, support, or resources to others, you create a network that is more likely to assist you when you need it most.

Tapping into the Hidden Job Market

Many job opportunities never make it to job boards or company websites, residing in what is known as the "hidden job market." These positions are often filled through word-of-mouth referrals. Networking gives you an inside track to these hidden gems, increasing your chances of finding your ideal job.

In today's dynamic job market, networking is an invaluable tool that can transform your job search. It is not just about collecting business cards or LinkedIn connections; it is about building meaningful relationships with people who can help you grow professionally and achieve your career goals. So, do not underestimate the power of networking. Invest time and effort in connecting with others, and you will discover that it is not only about finding a job; it is about building a successful and fulfilling career.

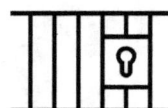

Chapter 8: Stay Out of Jail

"An individual who breaks a law that conscience tells him is unjust, and who willingly accepts the penalty of imprisonment in order to arouse the conscience of the community over its injustice, is in reality expressing the highest respect for the law." - Martin Luther King, Jr.

Liability

If you land in a low security comfortable prison, that will Situation your start-up. Do not do that!

As a business owner, you have a responsibility to provide quality and ethical services to your clients, and to protect yourself and your business from any legal or financial troubles. However, there are many variables that could push you and your company into contentious areas that could open you up to liability. Liability is the state of being legally responsible for something, such as damage, injuries, or losses, which may result from your actions or omissions as a business owner. Liability can have profound consequences for your reputation, credibility, and profitability, and may even lead to lawsuits or penalties.

In this chapter, I will discuss some of the common liability issues that start-up businesses may encounter, and how to avoid or reduce them. Will also share some real-life stories and examples to illustrate these issues and their solutions. Here are some of the topics that I will cover:

Scope of practice and expertise

This refers to the boundaries and limitations of your business services, based on your qualifications, skills, and knowledge. You should not provide services that are outside of your scope of practice or expertise, such as medical, psychological, legal, or financial advice, unless you are licensed or certified to do so.

Doing so may expose you to liability for negligence, malpractice, or fraud, and may also violate the ethical standards of your profession or industry. To avoid this issue, you should clearly define and communicate your scope of practice and expertise to your clients and refer them to other professionals when necessary.

You should also document your credentials, training, and experience, and keep them updated and relevant. Here is an example of how to manage this issue:

Story

Currently I am running a business that provides personal and professional coaching through career and executive coaching, and business psychologists. Sometimes our clients get confused between clinical therapy and coaching. Clinical therapy is typically focused on your past (childhood, and developmental stages) and mental health related. Juxtaposed to therapy, a coach is someone who works with you on your current situation and forward, where traditional therapy is about your past.

Most recently, I had a client who initially needed life coaching to help with some minor personal issues and she also needed advice on how to build healthy relationships and improve her healthy habits. So, I qualified (checked to see if I could help her) her and it appeared as though I could help her with life coaching. She began her life coaching sessions and then suddenly started asking questions about mental health, depression and medication and wanted to talk about her childhood and the abuse that she went through.

Lesson

Immediately at that point, the coach stopped the conversation and made a professional and empathetic request that the client hire a therapist to discuss those topics in more detail. The coach explained that they were not qualified or authorized to provide mental health services, and that coaching, and therapy are different in their goals and approaches.

The coach also provided the client with some referrals and resources for finding a suitable therapist. The coach then documented the conversation and the referral in their records and followed up with the client to ensure they were getting the appropriate help. Not only did this prevent liability issues when potentially working outside of our core capability, but it also protected the client's best interests and well-being.

Indeed, ensuring compliance with regulations such as HIPAA (Health Insurance Portability and Accountability Act) is crucial, especially in industries like healthcare where patient privacy and data security are paramount. It is essential to take proactive measures to protect your clients' sensitive information and mitigate potential liabilities. Here are some key steps to consider:

> **Staff Training:** Provide comprehensive training to all your staff, including coaches, on HIPAA regulations and the importance of maintaining patient privacy. Make sure they

understand the legal requirements and the severe consequences of violating HIPAA.

Ongoing Education: Keep your team updated on any changes or updates to regulations and/or compliance training. Regular refresher courses and awareness programs can help reinforce compliance.

Documentation

Maintain records of training sessions and certifications for compliance purposes. This documentation can serve as evidence of your commitment to compliance.

Data Security Measures

Secure Systems

Implement secure data management systems and protocols to safeguard patient information. Ensure that all electronic health records (EHR) and other sensitive data are encrypted and protected from unauthorized access.

Access Controls

Implement strict access controls to limit who can view and modify client data. Use strong passwords, multi-factor authentication, and role-based access permissions.

Regular Audits

Conduct regular security audits and assessments to identify vulnerabilities and address them promptly.

Monitor Client Status

Regular Check-Ins

Implement a system for regular check-ins with clients to monitor their status, needs, and any potential issues. This proactive approach can help identify and address concerns before they become significant problems.

Communication Channels

Establish effective communication channels with clients to encourage them to report any issues or concerns promptly. Ensure that clients are aware of your commitment to their privacy and security.

By following these steps, you can better protect your clients' sensitive information, reduce the risk of legal liabilities, and demonstrate your commitment to maintaining standards of privacy and security in your business operations.

Absence of Contracts

In the preliminary stages of my business, I made an unfortunate oversight - the absence of contracts or agreements with my clients. I thought that such formalities were unnecessary and overly complicated, and instead placed my trust in verbal or email confirmations. However, this decision would prove to be a mistake.

Over time, I began encountering various issues with some of my clients:

> **Payment Challenges:** Overdue payments and instances of non-payment became increasingly common, causing disruptions in my cash flow and creating financial stress.
>
> **Appointment Issues:** Cancellations and no-shows for scheduled business sessions disrupted my carefully planned calendar and adversely affected the progress of my clients.
>
> **Scope Creep:** Some clients expanded the scope of their requirements beyond the initially agreed-upon terms, resulting in additional work and time commitments on my part.

If you are curious what the number one thing is that kills a project, program, product development, its scope creeps. With a business like ours, that is based on intrinsic motivation, wanting to help others connect, wanting to feel good at the end of the day, you do have to set boundaries because people may want to take advantage of your generosity. It is a compliment if they try to take advantage of your generosity because it tells you that you are headed in the right direction.

Dissatisfaction

Occasionally, clients expressed dissatisfaction with the results of our business, leading to disputes and strained professional relationships. From my experience one of the best ways to head off client disputes is to stay in touch with your clients and develop an anonymous feedback form. If you clients are close to you, and have a vehicle to voice their dissatisfied, it can not only give you data, but also you will have clients who feel that they have a voice, and outlet to express their thoughts and feelings.

Through these challenges, I came to a stark realization: the need for clear and comprehensive contracts or agreements with my clients. Such documents are not only essential for safeguarding the interests of coaches but also for ensuring a positive and productive experience for clients. Decided to take proactive steps to rectify this situation. Here are the key actions I took:

Legal Expertise

Sought the guidance of a lawyer who specialized in business contracts. With their expertise, I began the process of creating a template that would encompass all crucial aspects of my business relationships. This template would serve as a foundation for my contracts with clients.

Comprehensive Coverage

The contract template was designed to address a wide range of essential elements, including:
- The scope of business services offered.
- Fee structures and accepted payment methods.
- Policies for cancellations and rescheduling.
- Confidentiality clauses to protect sensitive information.
- Clear definitions of intellectual property rights.
- Procedures for dispute resolution.

Tailored Agreements

Recognizing that each client's needs and goals are unique, I customized the contract template to align with the specific requirements of every individual client. This personalized approach ensured that the contract accurately reflected the expectations and commitments of both parties.

WARNING: POTENTIAL SITUATION

Having a lawyer do a lot of this work will be expensive. As of January 2024, lawyers have been charging anywhere between $200 - $3,000 an hour. Yes, AN HOUR! So, I strongly recommend that you do the groundwork and then give the lawyer a package of information, with your requests. For example, if you can cut down on some of the work, for example, by finding a sample contract to use, from a similar business, and using that to get ideas for your contract. Plus, it is a good thing to learn a little bit about contract law, for example, what can constitute an electronic signature. Remember working at an insurance company back in 2006 and they were starting to explore transforming their paper forms into online forms and allowing customers to sign their insurance documents online. It was a big debate, and now today, it is common.

As I have already explained, and it needs to be repeated, the path of entrepreneurship is not without its pitfalls. Understanding and preparing for the risks associated with starting a business is crucial. By forming an LLC and enlisting the help of a skilled business lawyer, you can significantly mitigate these risks. These steps are not just precautions; they are essential strategies for building a resilient and sustainable business. They provide a safety net, ensuring that the challenges you encounter on your entrepreneurial journey do not lead to irreversible consequences.

WARNING: POTENTIAL SITUATION

Now, the opposite of the previous warning, you do want your lawyer to understand your business, your customer base, and the services or products you are selling. If you were to get into a bad legal situation, the more they know about your business, the better they will be at defending it.

Integration with Online Booking

To streamline the process and enhance transparency, I integrated a feature into my website. Now, clients are required to review and electronically sign the contract or agreement before proceeding to book and make payments for their business sessions online. This step ensures that clients fully understand and consent to the terms and conditions governing my business services.

The Transformative Impact

Implementing these changes has had a transformative impact on my business. Here are some of the notable outcomes:

Enhanced Clarity and Communication

Contracts provide a clear framework for business relationships, reducing misunderstandings, and enhancing communication between myself and my clients.

Improved Financial Stability

With clear payment terms and policies in place, overdue payments and non-payment issues have significantly decreased, leading to improved financial stability.

Streamlined Operations

Clear guidelines on session scheduling and scope of work have resulted in more streamlined operations, reducing administrative complexities.

Legal Protection

Having legally binding contracts offers a layer of protection in case of disputes, helping to resolve issues in a more structured manner.

Legal Challenges and the Importance of Insurance

Despite having an LLC and legal counsel, start-ups can still face legal troubles that threaten their existence. Adequate insurance coverage becomes a lifeline in such scenarios. Types of insurance like general liability, professional liability, product liability, and cyber liability are crucial. They provide a safety net to cover legal expenses, settlements, or damages, thereby safeguarding your business and reputation.

Journey as a career coach has been marked by both successes and challenges. The absence of contracts and agreements with clients was a significant oversight, but it ultimately taught me a valuable lesson. Contracts are not just legal documents; they are essential tools for establishing trust, clarifying expectations, and ensuring the success of business relationships.

For coaches, both seasoned and aspiring, I highly recommend investing in the creation of comprehensive contracts or agreements. Seek legal counsel to tailor these documents to your specific business services and client needs. By doing so, you can protect your business, enhance client relationships, and ensure a positive and productive business experience for all parties involved.

In the dynamic world of business, contracts are the foundation upon which successful partnerships are built, fostering trust and accountability on the path to personal and professional growth.

Insurance and indemnity

These are the ways to protect yourself and your business from financial losses or liabilities that may arise from your business services, such as claims, lawsuits, or damages.

Insurance is a contract between you and an insurance company, where you pay a premium in exchange for coverage or compensation in case of a specified event or risk. Indemnity is a clause in your contract or agreement with your clients, where you limit or exclude your liability for certain events or risks, or where you require your clients to compensate you for any losses or liabilities that they cause.

You should consider getting insurance and indemnity for your business, as they can help you reduce your exposure to liability and provide you with peace of mind. To avoid or reduce liability issues, you should research and compare different types of insurance and indemnity options, such as general liability, professional liability, product liability, cyber liability, and more.

You should also consult with an insurance agent or a legal expert to help you choose the best option for your business.

The Crucial Lesson Learned

These experiences prompted a profound realization: the necessity of insurance and indemnity to protect both my business and the well-being of my clients. To address this need, I took several decisive actions:

Extensive Research

Embarked on an extensive research journey, exploring various insurance and indemnity options. These included general liability, professional liability, product liability, cyber liability, and more. Each option was carefully evaluated based on the unique characteristics of my coaching niche, the services offered, and potential risks.

Professional Guidance

Recognizing the complexity of insurance choices, I sought expert advice. Consulted with both an insurance agent and a legal expert who specialized in businesses. Their insights were invaluable in helping me select the most suitable insurance option.

Professional Liability Insurance

After thorough consideration, I opted for professional liability insurance. This coverage provided protection against claims and lawsuits arising from my coaching services. It covered various scenarios, including negligence, errors, omissions, and malpractice.

Indemnity Clauses

To further fortify my legal standing, I introduced indemnity clauses into my contracts and agreements with clients. These clauses limited or excluded my liability for specific events or risks, such as injuries, allergies, adverse reactions, or client dissatisfaction. Additionally, clients were required to indemnify me for any losses or liabilities they may cause, such as breaches of contract, defamation, or infringement.

Intellectual property

This refers to the creations of your mind, such as your ideas, inventions, designs, logos, names, or content, which have value and are unique to your business. Intellectual property is one of your most important assets, as it can give you a competitive advantage, attract customers and investors, and generate revenue.

However, intellectual property is also one of the most vulnerable and contested assets, as it can be stolen, copied, or infringed by others, such as your competitors, former employees, or customers. To avoid or reduce this risk, you should protect your intellectual property by registering it with the appropriate authorities, such as the U.S. Patent and Trademark Office or the U.S. Copyright Office, and by enforcing your rights and remedies, such as cease and desist letters, injunctions, or damages. You should also respect the intellectual property of others and avoid using or copying anything that you do not own or have permission to use.

Story

Theranos was a start-up that claimed to have developed a revolutionary blood-testing technology that could perform hundreds of tests with just a few drops of blood. The company raised over $700 million from investors and reached a valuation of $9 billion (about $28 per person in the US). However, it turned out that the technology was a fraud, and that the company had been using conventional machines and methods to conduct the tests. The company also faced allegations of patent infringement, trade secret theft, and false advertising, from competitors, former employees, and customers. The founder and CEO of Theranos, Elizabeth Holmes, was indicted on multiple charges of fraud and conspiracy, and faces up to 20 years in prison. *

Lesson

This story shows the importance of having a valid and original intellectual property, which can deliver what it promises, and that does not infringe on the rights of others. It also shows the consequences of lying and deceiving your stakeholders, and the potential criminal liability that you may face for doing so.

Contracts and Agreements

These are the legal documents that establish the terms and conditions of your business relationships with your stakeholders, such as your co-founders, investors, employees, customers, suppliers, or partners.

Contracts and agreements are essential for your business, as they can help you define and communicate your expectations and obligations, allocate your resources and responsibilities, and prevent or resolve any conflicts or misunderstandings. To avoid or reduce the risk of disputes or breaches, you should always have a written and signed contract or agreement with your stakeholders, and you should review and update them regularly. You should also make sure that your contract or agreement is clear, comprehensive, and compliant with the relevant laws and regulations.

Story

ZenPayroll was a start-up that provided online payroll services to small businesses. The company had a contract with one of its customers, Homejoy, which was a start-up that provided online booking for home cleaning services. The contract stated that ZenPayroll would withhold and remit taxes for Homejoy's cleaners, who were classified as independent contractors. *

However, Homejoy faced several lawsuits from its cleaners, who claimed that they were misclassified as independent contractors, and that they should have been treated as employees, with benefits and protections.

As a result, Homejoy owed millions of dollars in back taxes, penalties, and fees, and filed for bankruptcy. ZenPayroll was also sued by the IRS, which claimed that ZenPayroll was responsible for the unpaid taxes, as it was acting as Homejoy's agent. ZenPayroll denied the claim and argued that it was not liable for Homejoy's tax obligations, as it was only providing a service, and not a partnership.*

Lesson

This story shows the importance of having a clear and accurate contract or agreement that reflects the true nature and scope of your business relationship, and that protects you from the liabilities or risks of your counterparties. It also shows the importance of complying with the tax laws and regulations, and the potential civil liability that you may face for failing to do so.

To avoid or reduce the risk of violations or penalties, you should research and understand the compliance and regulation requirements that apply to your business, and implement the necessary policies, procedures, or systems to comply with them. You should also monitor and update your compliance and regulation status, and report or disclose any relevant information or incidents to the appropriate authorities, such as the FDA, FTC, SEC, or OSHA.

Story

Zenefits was a start-up that provided online human resources services to small businesses, such as payroll, benefits, and insurance. The company grew rapidly and reached a valuation of $4.5 billion (about $14 per person in the US). *

However, it turned out that the company had been violating various compliance and regulation rules, such as selling insurance without a license, falsifying insurance applications, evading insurance training requirements, and misleading investors and customers.

The company faced investigations and lawsuits from multiple state regulators, such as California, Washington, and Massachusetts, and was fined millions of dollars. The founder and CEO of Zenefits, Parker Conrad, was forced to resign, and faced criminal charges of fraud and conspiracy.

Lesson

This story shows the importance of complying with the compliance and regulation rules that apply to your business, and the potential legal and financial liability that you may face for violating them.

It also shows the consequences of cutting corners and compromising your integrity, and the potential criminal liability that you may face for doing so.

These are some of the common legal, financial, and liability issues that start-ups face, and how to avoid or resolve them.

Chapter 9: Push

"It does not matter how slowly you go, as long as you do not stop." – Confucius

Congratulations! You have made it to the concluding chapter of this book, where I will talk about how to keep your business growing and thriving overall. If you made it here and think that the challenging work is over? It is not, you need to keep pushing your business forward. This means being aggressive when fixing issues, monitoring your brand, and working on new lead generation sources. Whether your start-up is a success or a failure, you should never stop learning, improving, and innovating.

As a coach and an entrepreneur, you have a unique opportunity and responsibility to make a positive impact on yourself, your clients, and the world. To do that, you need to push yourself and your business to the next level and overcome any challenges or obstacles that may come your way.

In this chapter, I will discuss some of the key strategies and mindsets that can help you push your business to new heights and achieve your personal and professional goals. Will also share some inspiring stories and examples of coaches who have pushed themselves and their businesses, and the results and lessons that they have learned. Here are several topics that I will cover:

Innovation

This is the process of creating or implementing new or improved products, services, processes, or models, which add value and solve problems for your customers, your business, or your industry. Innovation is essential for your business, as it can help you stay relevant and competitive, differentiate yourself and your offerings, and increase your efficiency and effectiveness.

To foster innovation, you need to adopt a growth mindset, which is the belief that you can learn and improve your abilities and outcomes through effort and feedback.

"It's not about ideas. It's about making ideas happen." — Scott Belsky, co-founder of Behance

You also need to promote creativity and risk-taking, which are the abilities to generate and experiment with novel and useful ideas and solutions. In addition, you also need to build collaborative and diverse teams, which are groups of people who work together and leverage their different perspectives, skills, and experiences.

Story

A coach who has successfully innovated their business is Catherine B. Roy, who is the founder of LHM International, a business coaching company that uses artificial intelligence (AI) to simplify and enhance their coaching services.

Catherine, who has over 15 years of experience as a programmer, has integrated AI-powered tools into her business, such as chatbots, analytics, and automation.

These tools help her streamline and optimize her operations, such as lead generation, customer service, and performance measurement. They also help her deliver personalized and effective coaching experiences to her clients, such as tailored content, recommendations, and feedback. By using AI, Catherine has been able to grow and scale her business, achieve unprecedented results and satisfaction for herself and her clients. *

Lesson

This story shows the importance of leveraging technology and innovation to improve your business, and how you can use your existing skills and knowledge to create or implement new or improved solutions for your customers and your business.

Passion

This is the intense and positive emotion that you feel when you do something that you love, enjoy, or care about. Passion is vital for your business, as it can help you motivate and inspire yourself and your clients, overcome challenges and setbacks, and achieve fulfilment and happiness. To cultivate passion, you need to discover and pursue your purpose, which is the reason you do what you do, and the impact that you want to make on the world around you.

You also need to align your values and actions, which are the principles and behaviours that guide your decisions and actions, and that reflect your identity and beliefs. You also need to express your personality and vision, which are the traits and characteristics that make you unique and authentic, and the goals and aspirations that you have for yourself and your business.*

Story

Gina Lodge, who is the CEO of the Academy of Executive Coaching, followed her passion by founding a global coach training company for organizations and individuals. Gina, who has over 20 years of experience as a coach and a leader, has pursued her purpose of developing and empowering coaches around the world, and making a positive difference in their lives and careers. *

She has also aligned her values and actions, such as integrity, excellence, and collaboration, and has infused them into her business culture and practices. She made sure to express her personality and vision, such as being innovative, adventurous, and ambitious, and has created and shared her unique and authentic brand and message. By following her passion, Gina has been able to grow and lead her business and achieve success and satisfaction for herself and her clients.

Lesson

This story shows the importance of following your passion and doing what you love and care about, and how you can discover and pursue your purpose, align your values and actions, and express your personality and vision.

Persistence

This is the ability and willingness to continue doing something or trying to do something, even if it is difficult or challenging. Persistence is crucial for your business, as it can help you overcome obstacles and failures, learn from your mistakes, give feedback, and achieve your desired results and outcomes.

To develop persistence, you need to adopt a positive attitude, which is the way of thinking and feeling that focuses on the bright side of things, and that expects good and favourable outcomes.

Another idea is to set and pursue SMART goals, which are objectives that are specific, measurable, achievable, relevant, and time bound. You also need to seek and apply support and guidance, which are the resources and assistance that you can get from other people or sources, such as mentors, coaches, peers, books, or courses.

Story

Matt Ackerson demonstrated persistence as the founder and CEO of AutoGrow, a digital marketing and lead generation company for coaches and other businesses. Matt, who has over 10 years of experience as an entrepreneur and a marketer, faced and overcame many challenges and failures in his business journey, such as losing clients, running out of cash, and dealing with technical issues.

He learned and improved from his mistakes and feedback, such as pivoting his business model, optimizing his website, and hiring his team. He also sought and applied support and guidance, such as joining mastermind groups, reading books, and taking courses. By being persistent, Matt has been able to grow and scale his business and achieve his goals and dreams.

Lesson

This story shows the importance of being persistent and how you can adopt a cheerful outlook, set, and pursue SMART goals, and seek and apply support and guidance.

These are some of the key strategies and mindsets that can help you push your business to new heights and achieve your personal and professional goals. By following these tips and best practices, you can keep your business growing and thriving eventually.

BLOG POST

Embracing AI Technology: Preparing for the Future

Advancing your career, especially if you have more than 10 years of time left before retirement may require you to learn more about AI, because you will be affected by this innovative technology.

In an era defined by technological advancements, artificial intelligence (AI) has emerged as a transformative force that is reshaping industries and influencing the way I live, work, and interact. As AI technology continues to evolve at an unprecedented pace, it has become increasingly important for individuals, businesses, and societies to understand its potential and prepare for the future it promises.

The Power of AI Technology

Artificial intelligence refers to the ability of machines and systems to perform tasks that typically require human intelligence, such as understanding natural language, recognizing patterns, making decisions, and learning from experience. Unlike traditional computer programming, where explicit instructions are provided, AI systems learn and adapt from data, enabling them to improve their performance over time.

AI is already deeply integrated into our daily lives, from voice assistants like Siri and Alexa to personalized recommendations on streaming platforms and online shopping websites. Beyond these consumer-facing applications, AI plays a crucial role in sectors such as healthcare, finance, manufacturing, and transportation, optimizing processes, enhancing decision-making, and even aiding in scientific research.

Preparing for the AI Future

Embracing AI technology opens a world of opportunities. Businesses can leverage AI to gain insights from massive datasets, tailor customer experiences, automate routine tasks, and drive innovation. Individuals can acquire new skills that align with AI-powered tools and job roles, enhancing their employability and contributing to economic growth.

While AI brings immense potential, it also presents challenges that require careful consideration. Ethical concerns related to bias in AI algorithms, data privacy, and job displacement need to be guided by robust regulations and responsible AI development practices.

Preparing for an AI-driven future requires education and upskilling. Governments, educational institutions, and companies should collaborate to provide accessible training programs that equip individuals with the skills needed to work alongside AI technologies.

By investing in AI research and development, societies can foster innovation and maintain a competitive edge. AI-powered solutions have the potential to tackle complex problems like climate change, disease prediction, and resource optimization.

Businesses need to adapt their workforce strategies to accommodate AI integration. This might involve reskilling existing employees, redesigning job roles, and promoting a culture of continuous learning to ensure employees can collaborate effectively with AI systems.

Can AI Help Me Start a Business?

AI can be an asset for start-ups in many ways. AI can automate repetitive tasks such as data entry, customer service, and marketing, freeing up time for entrepreneurs to focus on more important tasks.

AI can analyse copious amounts of data and provide insights that can help entrepreneurs make better decisions. Plus, AI can help reduce costs by automating tasks and improving efficiency.

Regarding the customer experience, AI can help improve customer experience by providing personalized recommendations and support. And AI can be used to create new products and services for entrepreneurs who wish to diversify their offerings.

AI can also help optimize business processes by identifying inefficiencies and suggesting improvements and help start-ups attract investors by providing data-driven insights and demonstrating the potential for growth. Entrepreneurs must stay ahead of the competition by predicting trends and identifying emerging markets.

Education and Awareness: Governments and organizations should prioritize public education and awareness campaigns to demystify AI, dispel myths, and foster informed conversations about its benefits and risks.

Ethical Considerations: Developers must prioritize ethical AI design by addressing bias, transparency, and accountability in algorithms. AI should be developed to augment human capabilities, not replace them.

Regulation and Policy: Governments should work collaboratively with tech industries to establish regulations that safeguard against misuse of AI technology and ensure its responsible development.

Collaboration and Research: Encouraging collaboration between academia, industry, and government entities can drive innovation, advance AI research, and address emerging challenges effectively.

Inclusive Approach: Efforts to integrate AI should be inclusive, bridging the digital divide to prevent marginalized communities from being left behind in the AI revolution.

In conclusion, AI technology is a transformative force that can revolutionize our world. As AI continues to evolve, its impact will be felt across various sectors, from healthcare and finance to education and entertainment. By proactively preparing for the AI future through education, ethical considerations, collaboration, and responsible development, I can harness its potential to create a more efficient, innovative, and equitable society. The key lies in embracing AI as a tool to enhance human capabilities and shape a future that benefits all.

Final Thoughts

As I wrap up this book, I hope that my insights, experiences, opinions, and tips have equipped you with the knowledge and inspiration to embark on your business journey, with confidence and purpose. Whether you are just starting or looking to expand your business, there is a wealth of information and wisdom to guide you in your endeavours.

Starting and growing a business can be an exhilarating adventure, but it is not without its challenges and uncertainties. Along the way, you will encounter obstacles and questions, from finding your niche to navigating the intricacies of marketing, finance, and legal matters. You will need to strike a balance between your personal and professional life while taking care of your physical and mental well-being.

However, you need **not** navigate this path alone. There is a vast array of resources and tools at your disposal, from books and courses to podcasts, blogs, and software. Plus, contact CoreTactic, we can help guide you!

Seek guidance and support from mentors, coaches, peers, and potential partners who can offer valuable insights and encouragement. Learn from the stories and examples of successful business owners and entrepreneurs who have faced similar hurdles and achieved their aspirations.

In this book, I have covered essential topics to help you kickstart and advance your business, including:

- Discovering Your Passion and Purpose
- Understanding Your Target Market
- Creating and Delivering Business Services

- Being a Good Boss
- Marketing and Sales Strategies
- Financial and Operational Management
- Legal and Liability Considerations
- Sustaining Growth and Excellence
- Artificial Intelligence

As you embark on your start-up journey, remember that every step forward, no matter how small, is a stride toward your goals. Embrace the challenges, seize the opportunities, and always keep learning and growing. Your business has the potential to make a profound impact on the lives of others and bring fulfilment to your own. Best of luck and may your business endeavours be filled with success and fulfilment.

Thank you for reading this book, I am honored and grateful to share my knowledge and wisdom with you. Push yourself forward to help achieve your personal and professional goals.

Also, I would also like to invite you to join our community of coaches and entrepreneurs, where you can connect and network with other like-minded people and get access to more resources and tools that can help you grow your business. You can visit our website at coretactic.net to learn more and sign up.

APPENDIX A:

Small Business Dictionary and Acronym List

Here is a brief dictionary of common business terms and acronyms:

A

- **Accounts Payable (AP):** The amount of money a company owes to its vendors or suppliers for goods or services purchased on credit.
- **Accounts Receivable (AR):** The amount of money a company is owed by its customers for goods or services sold on credit.
- **Annual Report:** A comprehensive report on a company's activities throughout the preceding year, including financial statements and other relevant information.

B

- **Balance Sheet (BS):** A financial statement that reports a company's assets, liabilities, and equity at a specific point in time.
- **Business Plan:** A written document that describes in detail how a new business is going to achieve its goals.

C

- **Cash Flow:** The amount of cash and cash equivalents that flow in and out of a company.
- **Chief Executive Officer (CEO):** The highest-ranking executive in a company.

- **Chief Financial Officer (CFO):** The executive responsible for managing a company's financial operations.
- **Chief Operating Officer (COO):** The executive responsible for managing a company's day-to-day operations.
- **Cost of Goods Sold (COGS):** The direct costs associated with producing and selling a product or service.

D

- **Debt:** Money owed by a company to lenders or creditors.
- **Depreciation:** The decrease in value of an asset over time.
- **Dividend:** A payment made by a company to its shareholders, usually as a share of profits.

E

- **Equity:** The residual interest in the assets of a company after deducting liabilities.
- **Entrepreneur:** A person who starts and runs a new business.
- **Expense:** The cost of goods or services used to generate revenue.

F

- **Financial Statement:** A formal record of a company's financial activities.
- **Fixed Asset:** A long-term asset that is not expected to be converted into cash within a year.
- **Freelancer:** A self-employed individual who provides services to clients on a project-by-project basis.

G

- **Gross Profit Margin:** The percentage of revenue that remains after deducting the cost of goods sold.
- **Growth:** The process of increasing the size or scope of a business.

H

- **Human Resources (HR):** The department responsible for managing a company's employees.
- **Income Statement:** A financial statement that reports a company's revenues and expenses over a specific period of time.
- **Inventory:** The goods a company has on hand and available for sale.

I

- **Initial Public Offering (IPO):** The first sale of stock by a company to the public.
- **Interest:** The cost of borrowing money.

J

- **Joint Venture:** A business arrangement in which two or more parties agree to pool their resources for a specific purpose.

K

- **Key Performance Indicator (KPI):** A measurable value that demonstrates how effectively a company is achieving its key business objectives.

L

- **Liability:** An obligation that a company owes to others.

- **Limited Liability Company (LLC):** A type of business structure that combines the liability protection of a corporation with the tax benefits of a partnership.
- **Loan:** Money borrowed by a company that must be repaid with interest.

M

- **Marketing:** The process of promoting and selling products or services.
- **Market Share:** The percentage of total sales in a particular market that is held by a particular company.
- **Mission Statement:** A statement that defines a company's purpose and goals.

N

- **Net Income:** The amount of profit a company earns after deducting all expenses.
- **Non-Disclosure Agreement (NDA):** A legal agreement that prohibits the disclosure of confidential information.

O

- **Operating Expenses:** The costs associated with running a business.
- **Outsourcing:** The practice of hiring an outside company to perform a business function that is normally performed in-house.

P

- **Partnership:** A business structure in which two or more people share ownership of a company.

- **Profit and Loss Statement (P&L):** A financial statement that reports a company's revenues and expenses over a specific period of time.
- **Public Limited Company (PLC):** A type of business structure in which shares are publicly traded.

Q

- **Quality Control:** The process of ensuring that a product or service meets certain standards.
- **Quick Ratio:** A measure of a company's ability to meet its short-term obligations.

R

- **Return on Investment (ROI):** A measure of the profitability of an investment.
- **Revenue:** The income generated by a company from the sale of goods or services.
- **Risk Management:** The process of identifying, assessing, and mitigating risks that could negatively impact a business.

S

- **Small Business Administration (SBA):** A U.S. government agency that provides support to small businesses.
- **Sole Proprietorship:** A type of business structure in which an individual owns and operates a business.
- **Stock:** A share in the ownership of a company.

- **Start-up**: A new company that is just forming, and/or is established, but typically new and still operated by the original founder.

T

- **Trademark:** A symbol, word, or phrase that identifies and distinguishes a company's products or services from those of others.
- **Turnover:** The rate at which a company's inventory is sold and replaced over a specific period of time.

U

- **Unsecured Loan:** A loan that is not backed by collateral.
- **Utility Patent:** A type of patent that protects the functionality of an invention.

V

- **Venture Capital:** Money invested in a start-up or early-stage company with high growth potential.
- **Vertical Integration:** The process of a company owning and controlling all aspects of its supply chain.

W

- **Working Capital:** The amount of money a company has available to fund its day-to-day operations.
- **World Intellectual Property Organization (WIPO):** A United Nations agency that promotes the protection of intellectual property throughout the world.

APPENDIX B:

References*

Gallup. (2017). State of the American Workplace. Retrieved from https://www.gallup.com/workplace/238085/state-american-workplace-report-2017.aspx

Harvard Business Review. (2011). The Happiness Dividend. Retrieved from https://hbr.org/2011/06/the-happiness-dividend

LinkedIn. (2018). 2018 Workplace Learning Report. Retrieved from https://learning.linkedin.com/resources/workplace-learning-report-2018

Entrepreneur. (2019). How to Choose the Right Payment System for Your Business. Retrieved from https://www.entrepreneur.com/article/333448

Forbes. (2020). How To Choose the Best Payment Processor for Your Online Business. Retrieved from https://www.forbes.com/sites/theyec/2020/07/13/how-to-choose-the-best-payment-processor-for-your-online-business/?sh=3f1b4c7a6b5a

Shopify. (n.d.). How to Choose a Payment Gateway: 7 Questions to Ask. Retrieved from https://www.shopify.com/blog/how-to-choose-a-payment-gateway

Maybray, HubSpot, https://blog.hubspot.com/the-hustle/how-many-start-ups-fail , accessed January 2024

LegalZoom, https://www.legalzoom.com/articles/llc-asset-protection-how-to-protect-your-personal-assets-as-an-llc-owner accessed January 2024

CB Insights. (2022, December 1). Why start-ups fail: Top 12 reasons L CB insights. CB Insights Research. https://www.cbinsights.com/research/report/start-up-failure-reasons-top/

Entrepreneur. (2019). How to Create a Business Budget in 5 Steps. Retrieved from https://www.entrepreneur.com/article/334790

QuickBooks. (2020). How to Create a Business Budget: A Guide for Beginners. Retrieved from https://quickbooks.intuit.com/r/budgeting/how-to-create-a-business-budget

SCORE. (n.d.). How to Create a Business Budget. Retrieved from https://www.score.org/resource/how-create-business-budget

IRS. (n.d.). Small Business and Self-Employed Tax Center. Retrieved from https://www.irs.gov/businesses/small-businesses-self-employed

SBA. (n.d.). Business Taxes. Retrieved from https://www.sba.gov/business-guide/manage-your-business/pay-taxes

Bench. (2020). Small Business Taxes: The Complete Guide. Retrieved from https://bench.co/blog/tax-tips/small-business-taxes

Gracy, M. (2023) A quick guide to compliance for start-ups, Sprinto. Available at: https://sprinto.com/blog/compliance-for-start-ups (Accessed: 23 January 2024).

Dear Readers,

Personally, I would like to thank you for your interest in my book. Also, I would love to hear from you, receive feedback and suggestions for this book. You can contact me at https://coretactic.net, concierge@coretactic.net or call us at +1 952-452-1306.

I wish you all the best on your business journey and hope to hear from you soon.

To your best self,

[signature]

Nick Rustad, CEO, Co-Owner, and Founder of CoreTactic LLC

Nick is available for speaking engagements, please call his office at +1 612-268-5881 or email concierge@coretactic.net

About the Author

Nick's dad Vernon, his mom Audrey at his graduation from The College of Saint Scholastica in Duluth, MN. December 2014.

Hailing from the quaint town of Holyoke in northern Minnesota, my formative years were spent in Wrenshall, Minnesota, where I completed my elementary and high school education.

It is with immense pride that I share that I am the first member of my family to not only attain an undergraduate degree but also to achieve a master's degree.

Achieving a Bachelor of Science in Organizational Development from the College of Saint Scholastica in Duluth, Minnesota, and a Master of Business Administration (MBA) from the Carlson School of Management at the University of Minnesota, was a great thrill.

Throughout my career, I have had the privilege of working at or consulting with esteemed organizations, including The Pillsbury Company, Accenture, Perficient, Faegre Baker Daniels, LifeTouch, UCare, C4 Technical Services, The Bill and Melinda Gates Foundation, General Mills, SC Johnson, Kohler, U-Line, and many other companies.

The inception of CoreTactic marked the beginning of an exciting entrepreneurial adventure. Starting with just two manging members, my start-up has flourished and now boasts a team of sixteen experts individuals. CoreTactic is a personal and professional coaching organization committed to guiding clients through various life and career transitions. Our team comprises of expert life and career coaches, adept business strategy specialists, business psychologists, personal brand experts, and efficient placement services.

In closing, this work has been so rewarding and having my husband Travis with me has brought us closer! It is with immense pride that I continue to pursue my passion for coaching, helping individuals navigate the intricate path of life and career with confidence and purpose.

Inspiration Behind CoreTactic

Having worked in technology and leadership roles for over 25 years, I had a great run. However, in July 2023, I experienced something completely new – being laid off. This event caused me to go through anxiety and depression before I decided to turn this negative experience into something positive. After being handed a piece of coal, and I turned it into a diamond!

With the help of an executive coach and a personal brand expert, I was able to navigate through this transition successfully. During this time, I had an idea – what if there was an organization that offered a complete range of career and life coaching support, along with recruitment and placement services? All in one spot. If someone is going through a divorce and needs a new job, I can help. Recommend that this type of client meet with a life coach and a career coach, plus a session with a business psychologist.

"The way to get started is to quit talking and begin doing." – Walt Disney

At CoreTactic I help people get down to the **core** of their being, by teaching them **tactics** to improve their lives. And thus, CoreTactic was born.

Freebees!

For some low cost or free deals for your business, check out this list:

Betterment – one year of no fees and a high yield savings account (4.75%)
https://betterment.com/friend-referral-offer?referral_key=bmljaG9sYXNydXN0YWQ=

Buffer – social media scheduler
https://buffer.com/join/e8072385130ee1e8b0c60933e0b7d55fdca6688920251ac9f4091b41303db83c

Square – free payment processing up to $1,000
https://squareup.com/i/CORETACTIC

This page has been left intentionally blank.

www.ingramcontent.com/pod-product-compliance
Lightning Source LLC
Chambersburg PA
CBHW071056240526
45471CB00016B/1963